Italian Kids Songs & Rhymes

A Mama Lisa Book

Italian Kids Songs & Rhymes - A Mama Lisa Book

Original Material Written by Lisa Yannucci

Translations by Monique Palomares and Lisa Yannucci

Additional Translations by Our Many Correspondents

Compiled and Edited by Jason Pomerantz

Visit Mama Lisa on the web at www.MamaLisa.com

Contents

Introduction

Songs & Rhymes

18. Don don Dalena
(Dong Dong Dalena)
19. Dormi fili, dormi!
(Sleep Son, Sleep!)
20. Fa la ninna, fa la nanna
(Go to Sleep, Go to Sleepy)
21. Farfallina
(Butterfly)
22. Filastrocca della settimana
(The Days of the Week Rhyme)
23. Filastrocca senza senso - Ambarabai ciccì coccò
(Nonsense Rhyme)
24. Fra' Martino
(Frère Jacques)
25. Funiculì, Funiculà
26. Gesù bambino
(Baby Jesus)
27. Giro, Giro, Tondo
(Turn, Turn Around)
28. Il cavallo del bambino
(The Child's Horse)
29. Il mio cappello ha tre punte
(My Hat It Has Three Corners)
30. La Befana vien di notte
(The Befana Comes at Night)
31. La bella lavanderina
(The Pretty Washerwoman)
32. La gallina
(The Hen)
33. Lalla, Lalla, Lalla
34. La luna
(The Moon)
35. Le ciotoline
(The Little Bowls)
36. Lucciola, Lucciola
(Firefly, Firefly)
37. Mamma mia, dammi cento lire
(Mom, Give Me A Hundred Pounds)
38. Mano, mano morta
(Hand, Dead Hand)
39. Maramao
40. Maria lavava
(Mary Busy with the Washing)
41. Micio Miagolio
(Kitty Cat)
42. Mie Mama Mata Mata
(Coo-roo, Coo-roo)

43. Milano Torino
(Milan Turin)
44. Nanna cunetta
(As You're Sleeping in Your Bed)
45. Nella vecchia fattoria
(On the Old Farm)
46. Ninna nanna a sette e venti
(Lullaby At Twenty Past Seven)
47. Ninnananna di Fra' Simon
(Brother Simon's Lullaby)
48. Ninnananna di Gesù Bambino
(Infant Jesus' Lullaby)
49. Ninna nanna, ninna oh
(Lullaby, Lullaby, ooh)
50. Oh che bel castello
(Oh, What a Fine Castle)
51. Oh veni, sonnu
(Oh Come Sleep)
52. Peppina prendi un pettine
(Peppina, Get a Comb)
53. Personent hodie
(This Day Resounds)
54. Piazza bella piazza
(Plaza, Pretty Plaza)
55. Piva piva l'oli d'uliva
(Piva, Piva, Olive Oil)
56. Prezzemolo in mezzo
(Parsley Put Itself in the Middle)
57. Questo l'occhio bello
(This One, The Beautiful Eye)
58. San Nicolò de Bari
(Saint Nicholas of Bari)
59. Santa Lucia
60. Sedia, sediola
(Chair, Little Chair)
61. Sega sega mastu Ciccio
(Saw Saw, Master Ciccio)
62. Se sei felice tu lo sai
(If You're Happy and You Know It)
63. Seta moneta
(Silk Money)
64. Seta moneta (Filastrocca)
(Silk Money)
65. Sotto il ponte di Malacca
(Under the Malacca Bridge)
66. Stella, stellina
(Star, Little Star)

67. Sul tagliere l'aglio taglia
(Cut the Garlic on the Cutting Board)
68. Tacci e taccin
(Tacci and Taccin)
69. Tanti auguri a te
(A Lot of Wishes for You)
70. Te Didì
(You Little Finger)
71. Testa, spalle, ginocchia e piedi
(Head, Shoulders, Knees and Feet)
72. Topolino topoletto zum ba ba
(Mousie, Mousey Zum Ba Ba)
73. Trenta dì conta novembre
(Thirty Days Has November)
74. Trin' Trin', Cavallin'
(Trot, Trot, Little Horse)
75. Trotta, trotta, Bimbalotta
(Trot, Trot, My Horse)
76. Trotta trotta cavallino
(Trot, Trot Horsey)
77. Trucci Trucci Cavallucci
78. Turli Turli piangeva
(Turli Turli Was Crying)
79. Tu scendi dalle stelle
(You Come Down from the Stars)
80. Un elefante si dondolava
(One Elephant was Swinging)
81. Uno, Due, Tre
(One, Two, Three)
82. Un pezzo di pizza
(A Piece of Pizza)
83. Vinni la primavera
(Spring Has Come)

Thanks and Acknowledgements

About Us

Introduction

Italy! A land of beautiful art, great food and fascinating history. A land of spectacular natural scenery and lovely people. And a land with a rich tradition of children's songs and rhymes!

In this book we've gathered over seveny-five Italian songs and rhymes, presented in their original language and with translations into English. Many have commentary sent to us by our correspondents around the world.

You'll find nursery rhymes like *Batta le Manine* (Clap Your Hands), songs like *La bella lavanderina* (The Pretty Washerwoman) and Christmas carols like the beloved *Tu scendi dalle stelle* (You Come Down from the Stars).

Italy has been at the center of Western civilization for thousands of years, and we've included representatives from that entire time span. So you'll even find a few songs in Latin, the language of the Roman Empire and the Church, like *Personent hodie* (This Day Resounds), a carol from the 1500's.

We're also very pleased to include several songs in different Italian dialects. Italy has had varied linguistic influences over the ages and this has led to many different variants of the language still being spoken there. Many have also been preserved in immigrant communities, particularly in the US, though these are fading as the children and grandchildren of immigrants often speak only English. Yet those same people have treasured memories of the rhymes and songs their grandparents sang to them.

There's not always a sharp distinction between songs sung by children and by adults. So we've included a sampling of popular traditional songs like *Santa Lucia*.

At Mama Lisa's World we work with ordinary people around the globe to build a platform to preserve and exchange traditional culture. Most of the songs and rhymes featured here have been provided by our contributors, to whom we're very grateful! (Please see the Thanks and Acknowledgements section for a complete list of everyone who has contributed.) We love to receive new (public domain) material, so if one of your favorites has not been included please visit our website and write us to let us know.

The material presented here is part of a living tradition. So the version of a song you know may have some different words, or you may spell the dialect a little differently. Tell us about it! We consider our collection a dialogue and we update it all the time with your comments.

At the end of each item in this book, there's a web address to an online version of the song or rhyme. There we are often able to include sheet music, recordings and videos of performances.

We hope this book will help foster the love of the Italian language and culture all over the world!

Ciao,

Mama Lisa
(Lisa Yannucci)
www.mamalisa.com

Songs and Rhymes

1

A bi bo (A Be Bow)

A bi bo
(Italian Counting Out Rhyme)

A bi bo,
goccia di limone,
goccia d'arancia,
o che mal di pancia!
Punto rosso, punto blu,
esci fuori proprio tu!

A Be Bow
(English Translation)

A be bow*,
A drop of lemon,
A drop of orange
Oh, what a bellyache!
Red point, blue point,
Just you get out!

Notes

"A be bow" is a nonsense phrase for the sound.

For more about A bi bo, go to: http://www.mamalisa.com/?t=es&p=3345.

Arre, arre, cavalluccio (Giddy-up, Giddy-up Horsey)

This song is in the Neapolitan dialect.

Arre, arre, cavalluccio
(Italian Dialect Nursery Rhyme)

Arre, arre, cavalluccio
Quanne arrive a Murchigliano
Nce accattammo nu bello ciuccio
Arre, arre, cavalluccio.

Giddy-up, Giddy-up Horsey
(English Translation)

Giddy-up, Giddy-up horsey
When you get to Murchigliano
We'll buy a pretty donkey
Giddy-up, giddy-up horsey.

Notes

Melissa wrote: "My husband's grandmother (from Naples) sang this song to all the children, grandchildren and great-grandchildren... She just recently passed away and I have only JUST found the words to this great little bouncing rhyme. I only wish I had the song to go with the words now!"

-If anyone can help with the tune or if you can send a recording, please email me. Thanks! Mama Lisa

For more about Arre, arre, cavalluccio, go to:
http://www.mamalisa.com/?t=es&p=2734.

3

Aulì ulè

Here's "a Lombard 'conta' (i.e. a counting-out rhyme) that's very, very old.

It's completely nonsense: the words are non-existent either in Italian or in Lombard dialects." –Gian Carlo

Aulì ulè
(Italian Counting-out Rhyme)

Aulì ulè che t'amusè
che t'aprofita lusinghè.
Tulilèm blem blum
Tulilèm blem blum

Aulì ulè
(English Translation)

Aulì ulè che t'amusè
che t'aprofita lusinghè.
Tulilèm blem blum
Tulilèm blem blum

For more about Aulì ulè, go to: http://www.mamallsa.com/?t=co&p-3293

4

Avete paura dell'uomo nero? (Are you Afraid of the Bogeyman?)

"L'uomo nero" is the bogeyman. In Italian, the phrase literally translates to "the black man" because he's dressed in a long black coat with a hood hiding his face. ("Black man" has no racist connotations.) "L'uomo nero" doesn't usually harm kids, but he does take them away to a scary place. There's even a lullaby (http://www.mamalisa.com/?t=es&p=2168&c=120) where he takes them away for a whole year.

I asked Italian school teacher Emanuela Marsura about the "l'uomo nero" (the black man). Here's what she wrote:

"Our 'black man' (l'uomo nero) is a character of fantasy that every mother and father mentions to his child to persuade him he has to go to sleep or eat without a tantrum.

We also have a game about the 'black man'. Here's how you play it..."

Avete paura dell'uomo nero?
(Italian Children's Game)

UN GRUPPO DI BAMBINI SI METTE DAVANTI AD UN BAMBINO SOLO, POCO LONTANI. IL BAMBINO SOLO DICE A VOCE ALTA:

Bambino: "Avete paura dell'uomo nero?"

Gruppo: "Noooo!"

Bambino: "Volete vederlo?"

Gruppo: "Siiii!"

Bambino: "Venite!"

Il bambino "uomo nero" si gira intorno e fa finta di dormire.

I bambini toccano l'uomo nero e poi scappano.

I bambini cercano di non farsi prendere.

Quando l'uomo nero tocca un bambino, questo bambino è un prigioniero.

L'ultimo giocatore che rimane è salvo.

Egli diventa il nuovo uomo nero!

Are you Afraid of the Bogeyman?
(English Translation)

A GROUP OF CHILDREN STANDS IN FRONT OF A SINGLE CHILD, NOT FAR
FROM HIM/HER. THE CHILD WHO'S ALONE BEGINS BY SAYING OUT LOUD
THE FOLLOWING:

Single Kid: "Are you afraid of the bogeyman?"

Group: "Noooo!"

Single Kid: "Do you want to see it?"

Group: "Siiii!" (Yes!)

Single Kid: "Come on!"

The child "bogeyman" turns around and pretends to sleep.

The children touch the bogeyman and then they run away.

The bogeyman chases them and they try not to get caught.

When the bogeyman touches a child, that child is a prisoner.

The last player who remains is safe.

He becomes the new bogeyman.

For more about Avete paura dell'uomo nero?, go to:
http://www.mamalisa.com/?t=es&p=3346.

5

Batta le Manine (Clap Your Hands)

Here's a popular rhyme that has many different versions in both standard Italian and some dialects...

Batta le Manine
(Italian Fingerplay)

Batta le manine
Ora viene papà
Si prendere confitine
(baby's name) si mangerà!

Clap Your Hands
(English Translation)

Clap your hands
Daddy's coming home soon
He's bringing candy
(Baby) is going to eat it.

Game Instructions

On last line put baby's hands to mouth and say "ummummummumm"

For more about Batta le Manine, go to: http://www.mamalisa.com/?t=es&p=890.

6

Batti manuzzi (Clap Your Little Hands)

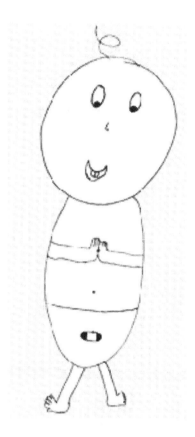

Batti manuzzi
(Sicilian Dialect Fingerplay)

Batti manuzzi ca veni Papa!
Poita cusuzzi e si nni va
Poita miennuli e nuchiddi
Pi accuiddari sta picciridda / (stu picciriddu)
Saleeeeeee!*

Clap Your Little Hands
(English Translation)

Clap your little hands because Daddy is coming!
He'll bring little things (gifts) and then he'll go.
He'll bring almonds and hazelnuts
To please his daughter / (son)
Saleeee!

Notes

A gleeful exclamation pronounced "salay". On that word, the hand goes up onto the child's face gently squishing the cheeks.

Here is the rhyme in standard Italian:

Batti manini che vieni Papa!
Porta cosine e se ne va
Porta mandorle e noccioli
Per accordare questa figliola / questo figliolo
Saleeeeeee!

For more about Batti manuzzi, go to: http://www.mamalisa.com/?t=es&p=3333.

Bobo la bilancia (Bobo the Scale)

"There is a rhyme my mother-in-law recited 40 years ago and there are still locals who know it but the final lines vary. The first four lines have a sort of See Saw Marjory Daw (http://www.mamalisa.com/?t=hes&p=1362) rhythm. I learnt this on the Island of Elba Tuscany and the nearest I can get on internet is Seta Moneta (http://mamalisa.com/?t=es&p=3101&c=120)." -Janet

Bobo la bilancia
(Italian Nursery Rhyme)

Bobo la bilancia,
il bimbo* è andato in Francia,
In Francia Gaeta,
ci sono le belle donne
che filano la seta,
La seta e la bambagia,
La seta e la bambagia,
Ambarabà si chiama
Maria Luisa che mangia
i fichi che son maturi
Insieme ai canguri.

Bobo the Scale
(English Translation)

Bobo the Scale,
The Child has gone to France
To France, Gaeta,
There are beautiful women
Who spin the silk,
Silk and cotton,
Silk and cotton,
Her name is Ambaraba,
Maria Luisa who eats
Figs that are ripe
Together with the kangaroos.

Notes

*or "babbo" = father
**Ambarabà is a nonsense word
(Note: there's a well-known rhyme called Ambarabà ciccì coccò
(http://www.mamalisa.com/?t=es&p=2193&c=120).)

For more about Bobo la bilancia, go to: http://www.mamalisa.com/?t=es&p=3283.

8

Bolli bolli pentolino (Boil, Boil, Little Pot)

*Some people sing this to the tune of Twinkle, Twinkle, Little Star
(http://www.mamalisa.com/?t=es&p=783&c=23) (though another tune is
sometimes used for this song)…*

Bolli bolli pentolino
(Italian Lullaby)

Bolli bolli pentolino,
fa la pappa al mio bambino;
la rimescola la mamma
mentre il bimbo fa la nanna;
fa la nanna gioia mia
o la pappa scappa via.

Boil, Boil, Little Pot
(English Translation)

Boil, boil, little pot,
Cook the food for my baby.
Mommy mixes it
While the baby sleeps.
Go to sleep, my joy,
Or your food will run away.

For more about Bolli bolli pentolino, go to:
http://www.mamalisa.com/?t=es&p=3299.

Capra Capretta (Goat, Little Goat)

Capra Capretta
(Italian Nursery Rhyme)

Capra, capretta,
che bruchi tra l'erbetta,
vuoi una manciatina
di sale da cucina?
Il sale é salato,
il bimbo é nel prato,
la mamma é alla fonte,
il sole é sul monte,
sul monte é l'erbetta,
capra, capretta!

Goat, Little Goat

(English Translation)

Oh goat, little goat
Who grazes in the grass,
Do you want a handful
of table salt?
Salt is salty,
The child's in the meadow
The mother's at the spring
The sun is on the mountain
The mountain is in the grass
Goat, kid goat!

Notes

"Sale" in the drawing means "Salt" in English.

For more about Capra Capretta, go to: http://www.mamalisa.com/?t=es&p=3328.

10

Centocinquanta (One Hundred and Fifty)

Emanuela wrote, "I teach my students this version of 'Centocinquanta', which is part of the rhyme 'Seta moneta (http://www.mamalisa.com/?t=es&p=3101&c=120)'..."

Centocinquanta
(Italian Counting-out Rhyme)

Centocinquanta
la pecora canta
canta il gallo
risponde la gallina
Madama Colombina
s'affaccia alla finestra
con tre colombe in testa
Passan tre fanti
su tre cavalli bianchi:
bianca la sella,
bianca la donzella,
addio mammina bella.

One Hundred and Fifty
(English Translation)

One hundred and fifty,
The ewe sings
The rooster sings
The hen answers.
Lady Columbine
Looks out the window
With three doves on her head.
Three infantrymen pass
On three white horses:
White, the saddle
White, the damsel,
Goodbye beautiful mommy.

For more about Centocinquanta, go to: http://www.mamalisa.com/?t=es&p=3103.

11

C'era una volta un Re (There Once Was a King)

This is a circular rhyme which can go on and on ad infinitum…

C'era una volta un Re
(Italian Nursery Rhyme)

C'era una volta un Re
seduto sul sofà
che disse alla sua serva
raccontami una storia

e la serva incominciò:

C'era una volta un Re
seduto sul sofà
che disse alla sua serva
raccontami una storia
e la serva incominciò:

C'era una volta un Re
seduto sul sofà
che disse alla sua serva
raccontami una storia
e la serva incominciò…

There Once Was a King
(English Translation)

There once was a king,
Sitting on the sofa,
He said to his maid
Tell me a story,
And the maid began:

There once was a king,
Sitting on the sofa,
He said to his maid
Tell me a story,
And the maid began:

There once was a king,
Sitting on the sofa,
He said to his maid
Tell me a story,
And the maid began…

For more about C'era una volta un Re, go to:
http://www.mamalisa.com/?t=es&p=3329.

12

Chi beddu stu cappiduzzu (How Beautiful is this Hat)

Chi beddu stu cappiduzzu
(Sicilian Dialect Nursery Rhyme)

Chi beddu stu cappiduzzu
Chi beddu saporito
Quannu mi l'ha mettiri
Quannu mi fazz'u zitu
Scinnu pi lu Cassuru
Scinnu pi li Banneri
E tutti chi me ricuni
Bongiorno cavaleri!

How Beautiful is this Hat
(English Translation)

How beautiful is this hat,
How sweet it is.
When do I put it on?
When I become engaged.
Going down to Cassaro Street*
Going down to Banneri Street*
Everyone who meets me
Says good morning sir**.

Notes

*Il Càssaro, aka Corso/Via Vittorio Emanuele is the oldest street in Palermo, Sicily.
Li Banneri (Via Bandiera) is another Palermo street famous for its stately mansions.
Ann originally translated the 5th and 6th lines as, "Going down to the barracks, Going down for the flags." We believe these lines are about two streets of Palermo.

**Gentleman, or soldier

Game Instructions

Rosaspina wrote that this nursery rhyme is sung at the table while eating a tangerine. (I'm loosely translating here...) Take a slice of tangerine with its peel on. Open it up and put it on your index finger like a hat and sing the rhyme. On the last line, "Bongiorno cavaleri!", have your finger bow and then put the tangerine in your mouth to eat.

Comments

Grazia wrote about this song on her site (http://lanonnadiinternet.spaces.live.com/blog/cns!4D5D863317A3A444!376.entr y) (here translated into English): "...it's about the story of a very beautiful hat to put on when one goes for a stroll around the most important streets of Palermo and for some special event like a new engagement."

For more about Chi beddu stu cappiduzzu, go to:
http://www.mamalisa.com/?t=es&p=2894.

There, you'll find a video performance.

13

Cimene, Cimene (Chimney, Chimney)

Cimene, Cimene
(Italian Nursery rhyme)

Cimene, cimene, cimene
Ci ste sus ?
O tenus !
Ci sta fa?
O frigge u pesc!
E la spine ?
A qui le da?
O gat!
Shitte gat, shitte gat, shitte gat.

Chimney, Chimney
(English Translation)

Chimney, chimney, chimney
Who is up there?
The chimney sweep!
What is he doing?
Frying fish!
And the spine?
Who gets that?
The cat!
Get out cat! Get out cat! Get out cat!

Game Instructions

All the participants put their hands one on top of the other's hands. As they chant the song they move one hand to the top of the stack of hands. When it comes to the last line they make the movement much faster whereby they end up slapping each others hands (not hard though).

Comments

Lois wrote me, "This is a Pugliese dialectical children's game. All the participants put their hands one on top of the others' hands. As they chant the song they move one hand to the top of the stack of hands. When it comes to the last line they make the movement much faster whereby they end up slapping each others hands (not hard though).

*Note. Little American kids love this chant not only because of the game but also because at the end they 'think' they are being naughty and saying 'sh*tty cat' with adult permission. You can explain, if need be, that 'Shitte gat' in dialect means 'uscite gatto' - 'Get out cat' . Personally I don't explain it to my American nieces and nephews because they get so much pleasure out of thinking they are saying a naughty, forbidden word.

Another cute linguistic story is that in Italian we always say 'Giu' to our cats when they jump up on tables (it simply means 'down' and is pronounced 'Jew'). Once an American Jewish friend of my daughter was visiting and the cat jumped up on the table and Tonia starting yelling 'Giu, giu' at the cat. Her friend mistakenly thought that in anger Tonia was calling the cat a 'Jew' for being naughty. Tonia, naturally explained."

For more about Cimene, Cimene, go to: http://www.mamalisa.com/?t=es&p=879.

14

Cincirinella

Cincirinella is a tarantella… which is a traditional style of Italian dance song with a fast upbeat tempo.

Cincirinella
(Italian Children's Song)

Cincirinella l'aveva una mula
tutto lo giorno la dava a vettura,
le metteva la briglia e la sella,
trotta, trotta, Cincirinella.

Cincirinella sul monte e sul piano
mai non cascava ed andava lontano.
Se di scudi portava un bel sacco,
trotta, trotta, non era mai stracco!

Cincirinella correva, correva,
cento chilometri al giorno faceva
e di notte seguiva una stella,
trotta, trotta, Cincirinella!

Cincirinella andava di fretta
e se ne stava seduto a cassetta,
non temeva ne pioggia ne vento,
trotta, trotta, cantava contento!

Cincirinella l'aveva una mula
tutto lo giorno la dava a vettura,
le metteva la briglia e la sella,
trotta, trotta, Cincirinella.

Cincirinella
(English Translation)

Cincirenella, his mule he would hire
Hitched to his wagon she never would tire;
When she was harnessed with saddle and bridle,
Trit-trot, trit-trot, they never went idle.

Over the plains, the mountains and hills,
He never fell off, he suffered no ills.
Whenever his sack was brimful of gold,
Trit-trot, trit-trot, he never felt old.

So Cincirenella went speeding away,
Hundreds of miles he would ride every day;
When the night fell he would follow his star,
Trit-trot, trit-trot, he traveled afar.

As Cincirenella went tearing along,
Atop of his box he'd be singing a song,
Blithely he'd brave both the wind and the rain,
Trit-trot, trit-trot, he'd sing his refrain!

Cincirenella, his mule he would hire,
Hitched to his wagon she never would tire;
Once she was harnessed with saddle and bridle,
Trit-trot, trit-trot, they never went idle.

For more about Cincirinella, go to: http://www.mamalisa.com/?t=es&p=876.

There, you'll find a video performance.

15

Dice il pollice (The Thumb Says)

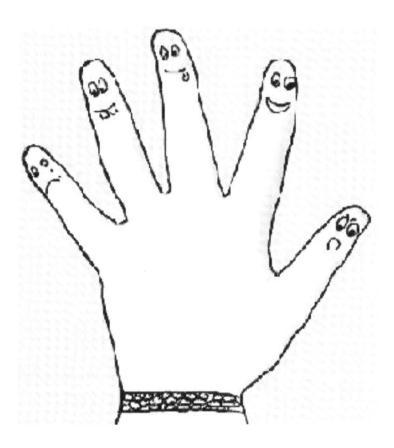

This Little Piggy in Italian...

Dice il pollice
(Italian Finger Play)

Dice il pollice: Non c'è più pane !
Dice l'indice: come faremo?
Dice il medio: lo compreremo

Dice: l'anulare: ce n'è un pezzettino
Dice il mignolo: datelo a me che sono il più piccolino.

The Thumb Says
(English Translation)

The thumb says, "There is no bread!"
The pointer says, "What will we do?"
The middle finger says, "We'll buy it."
The ring finger says, "There's a small piece."
The pinky says, "Give it to me for I am the smallest".

Notes

Anna Calise sent another version:

This Little Piggy (HTTP://WWW.MAMALISA.COM/?T=HES&P=129) IN ITALIAN...

Pollice dice non c'e' pane
Indice dice come faremo ?
Medio dice lo compreremo
Anulare dice, ma c'e n'e' un pezzettino
e Mignolo dice: dammelo a me che io sono il piu' piccino.

English Translation:

Thumb says, "There is no bread."
Index says, "What will we do?"
Middle says, "We will buy it."
Ring says, "There is a little piece."
And Pinky says, "Give it to me, because I'm the smallest."

For more about Dice il pollice, go to: http://www.mamalisa.com/?t=es&p=2539.

16

Din, Don, Campanon (Ding, Dong, Big Bell's Tones)

Din, Don, Campanon
(Italian Nursery Rhyme)

Din, don
campanon
quattro vecchie sul balcon:
una che fila, una che taglia,
una che fa i cappelli di paglia,
una che fa i coltelli d'argento
per tagliare la testa al vento.

Ding, Dong, Big Bell's Tones
(English Translation)

Ding, dong
Big bell's tones,
On the porch sit four old crones:
See one spin, see one snip without a flaw,
See the third shape hats of straw,
Silver knives the fourth makes dread
To chop off the cold wind's head.

Notes

Literal translation:

Ding, dong
Big bell
Four old ladies on the balcony,
One is spinning, one is cutting,
One is making straw hats,
One is making silver knives
To chop off the head of the wind.

For more about Din, Don, Campanon, go to:
http://www.mamalisa.com/?t=es&p=891.

17

Dona nobis pacem (Give Us Peace)

Dona nobis pacem means "Give us peace" or "Grant us peace". The phrase is sung as a round over and over again to form a song...

Dona nobis pacem
(Latin Round)

Dona nobis pacem

Give Us Peace
(English Translation)

Give us peace

Comments

This phrase is also part of the Catholic mass. The music is by W.A. Mozart.

For more about Dona nobis pacem, go to:
http://www.mamalisa.com/?t=es&p=2488.

There, you'll find sheet music, an MP3 tune and a MIDI melody.

18

Don don Dalena (Dong Dong Dalena)

Gayle sent me this Italian nursery rhyme with the note, "My grandparents, who were from the Abruzzi region (a miniscule town called Pratola), used to sing me this lullaby whenever they babysat. My mom was surprised to find me singing it one morning! I've looked all over the web and can't find it anywhere, not even on the Italian filastruccha site. This is my mom's recollection, phonetically (the Italian below)... I don't know Italian very well, and I know it's in dialect so the grammar is probably all wrong :) but it roughly translates to (the English below)..."

Don don Dalena
(Italian Dialect Nursery Rhyme)

Don don Dalena
Si morta Madelena
Chi se morta fa?
Ni voleva piu compa!

Dong Dong Dalena
(English Translation)

Dong dong Dalena
Madeline has died
Why did she die?
She didn't want to live anymore!

Notes

This song is in the Abruzzese Dialect.

If anyone can help with the correct spelling of the Italian, please email me. We also welcome for you to let us know if you're familiar with this rhyme or one similar to it. Thanks! -Mama Lisa

For more about Don don Dalena, go to: http://www.mamalisa.com/?t=es&p=1746.

19

Dormi fili, dormi! (Sleep Son, Sleep!)

"Dormi fili dormi" is from the point of view of Mary singing to the baby Jesus.

Dormi fili, dormi!
(Latin Christmas Song)

Dormi fili, dormi ! mater
Cantat unigenito:
Dormi, puer, dormi ! pater
Nato clamat parvulo:
Millies tibi laudes canimus
Mille, mille, millies.

Dormi, cor, et meus thronus;
Dormi matris jubilum;
Aurum caelestis sonus,
Et suave sibilum!
Millies tibi laudes canimus
Mille, mille, millies.

Ne quid desit, sternam rosis,
Sternam foenum violis,
Pavimentum hyacinthis
Et praesepe liliis,
Millies tibi laudes canimus
Mille, mille, millies.

Si vis musicam, pastores
Convocabo protinus;
Illis nulli sunt priores;
Nemo canit castius.
Millies tibi laudes canimus
Mille, mille, millies.

Sleep Son, Sleep!
(English Translation)

Sleep son, sleep! Mother
Sings to her only child:
Sleep, boy, sleep! Father at

The birth of the child cries out:
We sing praises unto thee a thousand times
A thousand, a thousand, a thousand times.

Sleep, my heart and my throne;
Sleep mother's jubilation
Who sounds like celestial gold,
sweet whistling!
We sing praises unto thee a thousand times
A thousand, a thousand, a thousand times.

I only need to lay thee on roses,
On a bed of violets,
On a floor of hyacinths
And a manger of lilies,
We sing praises unto thee a thousand times
A thousand, a thousand, a thousand times.

If you want music, I will summon
Shepherds at once;
No one is superior to them;
No one plays so purely.
We sing praises unto thee a thousand times
A thousand, a thousand, a thousand times.

Notes

The following was written about this song in 1881 in LITTELL'S LIVING AGE*:*
"There exists another Latin cradle song, not indeed dating from classical times,
but which, like the laconic effusion of the Roman nurse, forms a sort of landmark
in the history of poetry. It is composed in the person of the Virgin Mary, and was
in bygone days believed to have been actually sung by her. Good authorities
pronounce it to be one of the earliest poems extant of the Christian era…"

For more about Dormi fili, dormi!, go to:
http://www.mamalisa.com/?t=es&p=3272.

20

Fa la ninna, fa la nanna (Go to Sleep, Go to Sleepy)

Fa la ninna, fa la nanna
(Italian Lullaby)

Fa la ninna, fa la nanna
Nella braccia della mamma
Fa la ninna bel bambin,
Fa la nanna bambin bel,
Fa la ninna, fa la nanna
Nella braccia della mamma.

Go to Sleep, Go to Sleepy
(English Translation)

Go to sleep, go to sleepy
In the arms of your mother,
Go to sleep, lovely child,
Go to sleepy, child so lovely,
Go to sleep, go to sleepy
In the arms of your mother.

Comments

Gilbert wrote: " I would like to submit an Italian lullaby, 'Fa la ninna' which my mother used to sing to me. I am first generation Italian-American."

For more about Fa la ninna, fa la nanna, go to:
http://www.mamalisa.com/?t=es&p=1447.

There, you'll find sheet music, an MP3 tune, a MIDI melody and a video performance.

21

Farfallina (Butterfly)

Farfallina
(Italian Children's Song)

Farfallina
Bella e bianca
vola vola
mai si stanca
gira qua
e gira la
poi si resta sopra un fiore
e poi si resta spora un fiore.

Ecco ecco
a trovata
bianca e rosa
colorata
gira qua
e gira la
poi si resta sopra un fiore
e poi si resta spora un fiore.

Butterfly
(English Translation)

Butterfly
Beautiful and white
Fly and fly
Never get tired
Turn here
And turn there
And she rests upon a flower
And she rests upon a flower.

Here, here,
I have found her
White and red
Colored
Turn here
And turn there
And she rests upon a flower
And she rests upon a flower.

Photos & Illustrations

Comments

Nicole Midura had originally sent me this version:

Farfalline
(Italian)

Farfalline
bella e bianca
vola, vola,
mai si stanca.

Butterflies
(English)

Little butterflies
Beautiful and white
You fly and fly
And you never get tired.

Nicole wrote, "There are other verses to the butterfly song, but I can't remember them for the life of me."

Later I wrote Nicole asking about the differences in spelling between her version and a later one we received and she wrote me, "Since the songs were handed down from my mother it very well may be dialect. I speak both her dialect (which really amounts to a bunch of slang) and a bit of the 'perfect' form. The word 'farfalline' is already plural. The singular form would end in 'a'. That is why I changed the translation to Little Butterflies, instead of Little Butterfly."

By a happy coincidence I received the following version of "Farfallina" within a week or so of Nicole's version. This one was submitted by Lois Erskine. Here's it is...

Farfallina
(Italiano)

Farfallina bella bianca
Vola, vola mai si stanca
Gira di qua, gira di la
Fin che 'posa su Papà.

Butterfly
(English Translation)

Beautiful white butterfly
Without tiring, fly and fly
Turning here and turning there
Until she rests on Daddy's chest.

Lois wrote, "This is a song for young babies. The mother sings it while making little butterfly movements with her hand on the baby's tummy, legs, neck, face and arms. On the final line of the song she does the butterfly tickle on the baby's father."

Nina wrote: "I am first generation Sicilian. My Nonna used to sing this to me..."

Farfaletta bianca bianca
vuola vuola mai si stanca
gira di qua e gira di la

sopr' un fiore va posa.

White little butterfly
Flies and flies and never tires
Turns here and turns there,
And places herself upon a flower.

For more about Farfallina, go to: http://www.mamalisa.com/?t=es&p=874.

There, you'll find a video performance.

22

Filastrocca della settimana (The Days of the Week Rhyme)

Filastrocca della settimana
(Italian Nursery Rhyme)

Tanto sole Lunedì
bianca neve Martedì
Mercoledì si scende in piazza
per sentire la storia pazza.
Qui si ride il Giovedì
non si piange il Venerdì
e di Sabato vi avviso
c'è la festa del sorriso.
La Domenica è baldoria
perché inizia un'altra storia.

The Days of the Week Rhyme
(English Translation)

Lots of Sun on Monday
White snow on Tuesday
On Wednesday, one goes to the plaza
to hear the crazy story.
Hence one laughs on Thursday,
One doesn't cry on Friday
and on Saturday I inform you
that there's a festival of smiles.
On Sunday there's merrymaking
Because another story begins.

For more about Filastrocca della settimana, go to:
http://www.mamalisa.com/?t=es&p=3287.

Filastrocca senza senso - Ambarabai ciccì coccò (Nonsense Rhyme)

"'Ambarabà ciccì coccò' is also used as is 'one potato, two potato...........' to choose who is out!" -Janet

Gian Carlo wrote, "Regarding 'Ambarabai ciccì coccò ' (or 'Ambarabà ciccì coccò' depending on the version), it's a classical nursery rhyme that's many centuries old and it's still sung.

I've never heard an adult (parents and teachers included) complain about the line 'che facevano l'amore'. The fact is that the song is mechanically chanted as if it were nonsense. The lyrics only have a musical value, if we can put it this way. Kids (me too, when I was a little child, many years ago) recite it and do not think anything about. It is considered a sort of nonsense.

As you can check, you can find the rhyme on Wikipedia and if you search the Internet, you'll see that it's been copied or quoted in 20,600+ pages. That tells how famous it is and that it's not considered to be 'politically incorrect' as we'd say today.

There's even a web site called 'Ambarabai ciccì coccò' dealing with projects for preschool and kindergarten students."

Filastrocca senza senso (Ambarabai ciccì coccò)
(Italian Nonsense Rhyme)

Ambarabai ciccì coccò,
tre civette sul comò
che facevano l'amore
con la figlia del dottore.
Il dottore le chiamò,
ambarabai ciccì coccò.

Ambarabai ciccì coccò
(English Translation)

Ambarabai ciccì coccò*,
Three owls on the chest of drawers

That made love
With the doctor's daughter.
The doctor called them,
Ambarabai ciccì coccò.**

Notes

"Ambarabai ciccì coccò" is a nonsense phrase.
***A note. Of this rhyme other (very similar) versions exist, where, for example, the first and last verse are "Ambarabà ciccì coccò" and the fifth verse is "Il dottore si ammalò" (the doctor fell ill).*

*****

Gian Carlo also wrote: "As I said, this (ancient) rhyme is very famous in Italy. Umberto Eco, in 1992, wrote about it in 'Il secondo diario minimo' (a book about semiotics). Furthermore it is cited in songs, theatrical works etc. For example 'Tre civette sul comò' is the title of a theatrical piece that our famous actress Paola Borboni played in 1982; two songs played by children during 'Zecchino d'Oro' (a musical contest) remind one of this rhyme: 'Tre civette' (1965) and 'Barabà, Ciccì e Coccò' (1992). Vermondo Brugnatelli, an Italian linguist, in 2003 wrote a work, 'Per un'etimologia di am barabà ciccì coccò', about the etymology of the first verse."

For more about Filastrocca senza senso (Ambarabai ciccì coccò), go to:
http://www.mamalisa.com/?t=es&p=2193.

There, you'll find a video performance.

24

Fra' Martino (Frère Jacques)

The English translation is literal...

Fra' Martino
(Italian Children's Song)

Fra' Martino campanaro
dormi tu, dormi tu?
Suona le campane,
suona le campane,
din don dan
din don dan.

Frère Jacques
(English Translation)

Brother Martin, church bell-ringer,
Do you sleep, do you sleep?
Go and ring the bells!
Go and ring the bells!
Ding, dong, ding,
Ding, dong, ding.

For more about Fra' Martino, go to: http://www.mamalisa.com/?t=es&p=892.

There, you'll find sheet music, an MP3 tune and a video performance.

25

Funiculì, Funiculà

"Funiculì, Funiculà" was originally written in a Neapolitan dialect in 1880. Luigi Denza wrote the music and Peppino Turco wrote the lyrics. It was composed for the opening of the first funicular on Mount Vesuvius.

A funicular is an inclined railway that goes up a steep slope like a mountain. One tram goes up while another one goes down on a cable. They thereby counterbalance each other.

The funicular this song was celebrating was destroyed by an eruption of Mount Vesuvius in 1944.

The first English translation below is a loose one I did based on one on Wikipedia. The second English translation is not literal. It's the popular lyrics of "Funiculi Funicula" in English.

Funiculì, Funiculà
(Italian Dialect Traditional Song)

Aieressera, oì Nanninè, me ne sagliette,
tu saie addò tu saie addò
Addò 'stu core 'ngrato cchiù dispietto
farme nun pò!
Addò lo fuoco coce, ma si fuie
te lassa sta!
E nun te corre appriesso, nun te struie,
'ncielo a guardà!...
Jammo, jammo 'ncoppa, jammo jà,
funiculì, funiculà!

Nè... jammo da la terra a la montagna! no
passo nc'è!
Se vede Francia, Proceta e la Spagna...
Io veco a tte!
Tirato co la fune, ditto 'nfatto,
'ncielo se va..
Se va comm' 'à lu viento a l'intrasatto, guè,
saglie sà!
Jammo, jammo 'ncoppa, jammo jà,
funiculì, funiculà!

Se n' 'è sagliuta, oì nè, se n' 'è sagliuta la
capa già!
È gghiuta, pò è turnata, pò è venuta...
sta sempe ccà!
La capa vota, vota, attuorno, attuorno,
attuorno a tte!
Sto core canta sempe
nu taluorno
Sposammo, oì nè!
Jammo, jammo 'ncoppa, jammo jà,
funiculì, funiculà!

Funiculì, Funiculà
(English Translation)

Yesterday evening, Anna, I went up,
Do you know where?
Where this ungrateful heart cannot spite me any more!
Where the fire burns, but if you flee
It lets you be!
And it doesn't chase you, it doesn't burn you, to see the sky!
Let's go up to the top, let's go,
Funicular up, funicular down!

Let's go from the earth to the mountaintop!
Without walking!
We can see France, Procida and Spain...
and I can see you!
Pulled by a rope, no sooner said than done,
We'll go to heaven...

It goes like the wind suddenly,
Up, up, up!
Let's go up to the top, let's go,
Funicular up, funicular down!

We've climbed it, my love, we've already climbed
To the top!
It's gone up, then returned, then it's back...
It's always here!
The summit revolves, around, around,
around you!
This heart always sings, my love,
Let's get married one day!
Let's go up to the top, let's go,
Funicular up, funicular down!

Notes

Traditional English Version, translated/created by Edward Oxenford (circa 1888):

Funiculi Funicula

1. Some think the world is made for fun and frolic,
And so do I! And so do I!
Some think it well to be all melancholic,
To pine and sigh; to pine and sigh.

But I, I love to spend my time in singing,
Some joyous song, some joyous song,
To set the air with music bravely ringing
Is far from wrong! Is far from wrong!

(Chorus)
Listen, listen, echoes sound afar!
Listen, listen, echoes sound afar!
Funiculì, funiculà,
Funiculì, funiculà!
Echoes sound afar,
Funiculì, funiculà!

2. Some think it wrong to set the feet a-dancing,
But not so I! But not so I!
Some think that eyes should keep from coyly glancing,
Upon the sly! Upon the sly!

But, oh! To me the mazy dance is charming,
Divinely sweet! Divinely sweet!
And surely there is naught that is alarming
In nimble feet! In nimble feet!

(Chorus)

3. Ah me! 'tis strange that some should take to sighing,
And like it well! And like it well!
For me, I have not thought it worth the trying,
So cannot tell! So cannot tell!

With laugh, with dance and song the day soon passes
Full soon is gone, full soon is gone,
For mirth was made for joyous lads and lasses
To call their own! To call their own!

(Final Chorus)
Listen, listen, hark the soft guitar!
Listen, listen, hark the soft guitar!
Funiculì, funiculà, funiculì, funiculà!
Hark the soft guitar, funiculì, funiculà!

Here's the song in Italian:

Ieri sera, Annina, me ne salii,
tu sai dove?
Dove questo cuore ingrato non può farmi più dispetto!
Dove il fuoco scotta, ma se fuggi ti lascia stare!
E non ti corre appresso, non ti stanca,
a guardare in cielo!...
Andiamo su, andiamo andiamo,
funiculì, funiculà!

Ne'...Andiamo dalla terra alla montagna!
Non c'è un passo!
Si vede Francia, Procida e la Spagna...Io vedo te!
Tirati con la fune, detto e fatto, in cielo si va.
Si va come il vento all'improvviso, sali sali!
Andiamo, andiamo su, andiamo, andiamo,
funiculì, funiculà!

Se n'e' salita, Annina, se n'è salita
la testa già! È andata, poi è tornata,
poi è venuta... sta sempre qua!
La testa gira, gira, intorno, intorno, intorno a te!
Questo cuore canta sempre un giorno Sposami, Annina!
Andiamo su, andiamo, andiamo,
funiculì, funiculà! funiculì, funiculà!

For more about Funiculì, Funiculà, go to:
http://www.mamalisa.com/?t=es&p=2351.

There, you'll find a video performance.

26

Gesù bambino (Baby Jesus)

This carol is mainly in Italian, but the line, "Venite adoremus Dominum" is Latin.

The English translation is literal. There's a popular non-literal version of this song that's sung in English that you can find in the notes.

Gesù bambino
(Italian Christmas Carol)

Nell'umile capanna
nel freddo e povertà
é nato il Santo pargolo
che il mondo adorerà.

Osanna, osanna cantano
con giubilante cor
i tuoi pastori ed angeli
o re di luce e amor.

Venite adoremus
venite adoremus
venite adoremus
Dominum.

O bel bambin non piangere
non piangere, Redentor!
la mamma tua cullandoti
ti bacia, O Salvator.

Osanna, osanna cantano
con giubilante cor
i tuoi pastori ed angeli
o re di luce e amor.

Venite adoremus
venite adoremus
venite adoremus
Dominum.

Ah! venite adoremus
Ah! adoremus Dominum
venite, venite

venite adoremus
adoremus
Dominum.

Baby Jesus
(English Translation)

In the humble hut,
In cold and poverty
The Holy infant is born
That the world will adore.

Hosanna, hosanna*, sing
With a joyous heart
Your shepherds and angels,
O king of light and love.

Come let us adore,
Come let us adore,
Come let us adore
The Lord.

O beautiful boy do not cry
Do not cry, Redeemer!
Your mother cradles you,
Kisses you, O Savior.

Hosanna, hosanna*, sing
With a joyous heart
Your shepherds and angels,
O king of light and love.

Come let us adore,
Come let us adore,
Come let us adore
The Lord.

Oh! Come let us adore,
Oh! Come let us adore,
Come, come,
Come let us adore,
Let us adore
The Lord.

Notes

Hosanna is a shout of praise to God or Jesus.

Composed by Pietro Yon in 1917.

Comments

Here's the version that's normally sung in English (listen to an mp3 here (http://www.mamalisa.com/mp3/gesu_bambino_lib.mp3)). It was translated by Frederick H. Martens. The tune and lyrics of the chorus are used in the English Carol "O Come All Ye Faithful (http://en.wikipedia.org/wiki/Adeste_Fideles)".

When blossoms flowered 'mid the snows
Upon a winter night
Was born the Child, the Christmas Rose
The King of Love and Light.

The angels sang, the shepherds sang
The grateful earth rejoiced
And at His blessed birth the stars
Their exultation voiced.

(Chorus)
O come let us adore Him
O come let us adore Him
O come let us adore Him
Christ the Lord.

Again the heart with rapture glows
To greet the holy night
That gave the world its Christmas Rose
Its King of Love and Light.

Let ev'ry voice acclaim His name
The grateful chorus swell
From paradise to earth He came
That we with Him might dwell.

(Chorus)
O come let us adore Him
O come let us adore Him
O come let us adore Him
Christ the Lord.

For more about Gesù bambino, go to: http://www.mamalisa.com/?t=es&p=3313.

There, you'll find a video performance.

27

Giro, Giro, Tondo (Turn, Turn Around)

Giro, Giro, Tondo
(Italian Children's Song)

Giro Giro Tondo,
Quanto è bello il mondo!
Cento, cinquanta,
La gallina canta.
Canta da sola,
Non vuole andare a scuola.
Ma la scuola è tanto bella.
Canta canta gallinella!

Turn, Turn Around
(English Translation)

Turn, turn around,
How beautiful the world is!
One-hundred, fifty,
The hen sings.
She sings by herself,
She doesn't want to go to school.
But the school is so pretty.
Sing, sing little hen.

Notes

Annalisa from Brescia, Italy, wrote me in February 2005, "I'd like to send you the "Giro giro tondo" song that I sang as a child in the late sixties:"

Giro giro tondo
(2nd Version)

Giro giro tondo
Casca il mondo
Casca la terra
Tutti giù per terra.

English Translation

Turn, turn around
The world is falling down
The earth is falling down
Everybody's sitting down!

AT THE END EVERY CHILD SITS ON THE FLOOR = TERRA = EARTH.

Comments

Here's a version sent by Anna Simonetti with the note: "My name is Anna, I'm from Foggia and I'm sending you the version of Giro tondo that I sang as a child in the mid 60's…. -warm greetings."

Giro giro tondo
cavallo impero tondo
cento cinquanta
la gallina canta,
canta sola sola
non vuole andare a scuola.
La gallina bianca e nera
ci da la buona sera
buona sera buona notte
il lupo dietro la porta.

ENGLISH TRANSLATION:

Turn, turn around,
Horse, empire, circle
One-hundred fifty,
The hen sings.
She sings all alone,
She doesn't want to go to school.
The black and white hen
Bids us good evening,
Good evening, good night,
The wolf at the door.

Here's another version we were sent:

Giro tondo dei nipotini di Mussolini
Giro giro tondo
il mondo e' tondo
se viene un'altra guerra anche nonno cade a terra.

English Translation (by Monique):

Turn Round Mussolini's Small Grandchildren
Turn, turn, round
The world is round
If there's another war, even Granddad will fall* on the ground.

Literally "falls" - this includes the idea of loosing the war.

For more about Giro, Giro, Tondo, go to:
http://www.mamalisa.com/?t=es&p=888.

There, you'll find sheet music, a MIDI melody and a video performance.

28

Il cavallo del bambino (The Child's Horse)

Il cavallo del bambino
(Italian Lap Rhyme)

Il cavallo del bambino
va pianino, va pianino.
Il cavallo del vecchietto
va zoppetto, va zoppetto.
Il caval del giovanotto
va di trotto, va di trotto.
Il caval del mio compare
come il vento sa volare.

The Child's Horse
(English Translation)

The child's horse
Goes a-walking, goes a-walking.
The old man's horse
Goes a-limping, goes a-limping.
The young man's horse
Goes a-trotting, goes a-trotting.
My buddy's horse
Knows how to fly like the wind.

For more about Il cavallo del bambino, go to:
http://www.mamalisa.com/?t=es&p=3347.

29

Il mio cappello ha tre punte (My Hat It Has Three Corners)

Il mio cappello ha tre punte
(Italian Children's Song)

Il mio cappello ha tre punte
ha tre punte il mio cappello
e se non avesse tre punte
non sarebbe il mio cappello.

My Hat It Has Three Corners
(English Translation)

My hat it has three corners
Three corners has my hat
And had it not three corners,
It would not be my hat.

For more about Il mio cappello ha tre punte, go to:
http://www.mamalisa.com/?t=es&p=1781.

There, you'll find a MIDI melody.

30

La Befana vien di notte (The Befana Comes at Night)

The Befana brings toys to the Italian children during Epiphany night (the word "befana" comes from the word "epifania")

La Befana vien di notte
(Italian Befana Rhyme)

La Befana vien di notte
con le scarpe tutte rotte
col cappello alla romana
viva viva la Befana!

The Befana Comes at Night
(English Translation)

The Befana comes at night
In worn out shoes
Dressed like a Roman
Long live the Befana!

Notes

This rhyme is chanted.

Comments

Maria Sabatino-Cabardo sent us this version from Roseto Valfortore, a little mountain town in Puglia:

La Befana vien di notte,
con le scarpe tutte rotte,
ai bambini piccolini, lascia tanti cioccolatini
ai bambini cativoni, lascia cenere e carboni.

Translation

The Befana comes at night
In worn-out shoes
To the little children she leaves a lot of little chocolates
To the bad little children she leaves ashes and coal

You can read more about La Befana in Italy on Mama Lisa's Blog
(http://www.mamalisa.com/blog/in-italy-on-january-6th-befana-comes-with-gift-
for-kids-for-the-epiphany/)

For more about La Befana vien di notte, go to:
http://www.mamalisa.com/?t=es&p=3102.

There, you'll find a video performance.

31

La bella lavanderina (The Pretty Washerwoman)

Imitate the actions in the song…

La bella lavanderina
(Italian Children's Game Song)

La bella lavanderina
che lava i fazzoletti
per i poveretti
della città.
Fai un salto,
fanne un altro,
fai la giravolta,
falla un'altra volta,
guarda in su
guarda in giù
dai un bacio
a chi vuoi tu.

The Pretty Washerwoman
(English Translation)

The beautiful washerwomen
washing the hankies
for the poor
in the city.
Take a jump,
take another,
turn around,
turn again,
look up
look down,
give a kiss
to whoever you want.

For more about La bella lavanderina, go to:
http://www.mamalisa.com/?t=es&p=3327.

There, you'll find a video performance.

32

La gallina (The Hen)

La gallina
(Italian Children's Song)

Io avevo, io avevo una gallina
Dalla piuma, dalla piuma morbidina,
Dalla sera alla mattina
Lei cantava, lei cantava così ben.
Corococococo, corococococo,
Corococococo, corocococodè !

Ma un giorno, ma un giorno torno a casa,
Più non trovo, più non trovo la gallina
Che cantava poverina,
Che cantava, che cantava così ben.
Corococococo, corococococo,
Corococococo, corocococodè !

Io domando, io domando alla mia mamma
Dove è andata a finire la gallina.
- È in pignatta che cucina
Che cucina, che cucina così ben.
corococococo, corococococo,
Corococococo, corocococodè !

Ve lo giuro, ve lo giuro amici cari,
Che ho pianto, che ho pianto disperata,
Però quando l'ho mangiata:
Ma che buona, ma che buona , oh là là !

The Hen
(English Translation)

I had, I had a hen
With feathers, with feathers so soft
From evening to morning
She sang, she sang so well...
Corococococo, corococococo,
Corococococo, corocococodee!

But one day, but one day I came back home

I couldn't find, I couldn't find the hen
Who sang, poor dear,
Who sang, who sang so well...
Corococococo, corococococo,
Corococococo, corocococodee!

I asked, I asked my mommy,
Where had the hen gone.
"It's in the pot that simmers,
That simmers, that simmers so well"
Corococococo, corococococo,
Corococococo, corocococodee!

I swear to you, I swear to you dear friends,
That I cried, that I cried, desperately,
But when I ate it,
How good it was, how good it was, oh là là !

For more about La gallina, go to: http://www.mamalisa.com/?t=es&p=2169.

There, you'll find sheet music and a MIDI melody.

33

Lalla, Lalla, Lalla

Many sources on the internet and in print say this is likely to be the oldest lullaby. It's from ancient Rome. We believe the Sumerian "Lullaby For a Son of Šulgi (http://mamalisa.com/?t=es&p=520&c=84)" is truly the oldest known cradle song.

Lalla, Lalla, Lalla
(Latin Lullaby)

Lalla, Lalla, Lalla,
aut dormi, aut lacta

Lalla, Lalla, Lalla
(English Translation)

Lalla, Lalla, Lalla,
Either sleep, or nurse*.

Notes

Meaning "breastfeed"

Comments

No one is sure if the lyrics above make up the whole lullaby. They may be just the first two lines.

For more about Lalla, Lalla, Lalla, go to:
http://www.mamalisa.com/?t=es&p=3253.

34

La luna (The Moon)

La luna
(Italian Counting-out Rhyme)

La luna è una ruota gialla,
cade in mare e resta a galla,
gettano le reti i pescatori,
noi siamo dentro e tu sei fuori.

The Moon
(English Translation)

The moon's a yellow wheel,
It falls into the sea and remains afloat,
The fishermen cast their nets,
We're in and you're out.

For more about La luna, go to: http://www.mamalisa.com/?t=es&p=3285.

35

Le ciotoline (The Little Bowls)

Gian Carlo wrote me, "'Le ciotoline' means 'little bowls' ('ciotola' is a sort of cup)." The first line refers to joining your hands to make a cup or bowl to get water to drink (from the brook). That's what "do the little bowls" means in the second line.

Le ciotoline
(Italian Children's Song)

Uniamo le manine,
facciam le ciotoline:
l'acqua del ruscello
ci disseterà.

Tra là là là
tra là là là
tra là là là là là là.
Tra là là là
tra là là là
tra là là là là là là.

Se vuoi vedere bene
puoi fare il cannocchiale:
gli omini sulla luna
vedremo camminare.

Tra là là là
tra là là là
tra là là là là là là.
Tra là là là
tra là là là
tra là là là là là là.

The Little Bowls
(English Translation)

Let's join our hands,
Let's do the little bowls:
The water of the brook
Will quench our thirst.

Tra la la la
tra la la la
tra la la la la la la.
Tra la la la
tra la la la
tra la la la la la la.

If you want to see well
You can make a spyglass:
Little men on the moon
We'll see walk.

Tra la la la
tra la la la
tra la la la la la la.
Tra la la la
tra la la la
tra la la la la la la.

For more about Le ciotoline, go to: http://www.mamalisa.com/?t=es&p=2194.

There, you'll find sheet music and an MP3 tune.

36

Lucciola, Lucciola (Firefly, Firefly)

Ernestine Shargool wrote, "This rhyme is from Tuscany, but is known all over Italy in many different versions. Children recite these rhymes while chasing fireflies on warm summer evenings. In some areas there is the custom that when children catch a firefly they put it under an upside down glass before going to bed; in the morning they find that the firefly has left some money under the glass."

Lucciola, Lucciola
(Italian Nursery Rhyme)

Lucciola lucciola, gialla gialla
metti la briglia alla cavalla
che la vuole il figlio del re
lucciola lucciola vieni con me.

Firefly, Firefly
(English Translation)

Firefly, firefly, yellow and bright
Bridle the filly under your light,
The son of the king is ready to ride,
Firefly, firefly, fly by my side.

Notes

*****

Gian Carlo wrote, "About the rhyme 'Lucciola lucciola', the following is the version chanted here in Lombardy:

Lucciola lucciola vien da me:
ti darò il pan del Re,
pan del Re e della Regina.
Lucciola, lucciola, vien vicina.

ENGLISH TRANSLATION

Firefly, firefly come to me:

I'll give you some King's bread,
Some King and Queen's bread.
Firefly, firefly, come near to me."

For more about Lucciola, Lucciola, go to:
http://www.mamalisa.com/?t=es&p=875.

37

Mamma mia, dammi cento lire (Mom, Give Me A Hundred Pounds)

This song is from the northern Italy and dates back to the 1800's. The author is unknown. It's said to be inspired by the ballad, "Maledizione della madre" ("The Mother's Doom").

Mamma mia, dammi cento lire
(Italian Traditional song)

Mamma mia, dammi cento lire
che in America voglio andar
mamma mia dammi cento lire
che in America voglio andar

Cento lire io te le do
ma in America no no no
cento lire io te le do
ma in America no no no

Suoi fratelli alla finestra
mamma mia, lasciala andar
suoi fratelli alla finestra
mamma mia, lasciala andar

Pena giunti in alto mare
bastimento si ribaltò
pena giunti in alto mare
bastimento si ribaltò

I miei capelli son ricci e belli
l'acqua del mare li marcirà
i miei capelli son ricci e belli
l'acqua del mare li marcirà

Le parole dei miei fratelli
sono quelle che m'àn tradì
le parole dei miei fratelli
sono quelle che m'àn tradì

Le parole della mamma
sono venute la verità

le parole della mamma
sono venute la verità.

Mom, Give Me A Hundred Pounds
(English Translation)

Oh Mom, give me a hundred pounds,
To America I want to go.
Oh mom give me a hundred pounds,
To America I want to go.

A hundred pounds I give them...
But to America no no no.
A hundred pounds I give them to you,
But to America no no no.

Her brothers at the window,
Oh mom, let her go.
Her brothers at the window,
Oh mom, let her go.

Just arriving on the high seas,
The ship is reversed.
While arriving on the high seas,
The ship is reversed.

My hair is curly and beautiful,
In sea water it will rot.
My hair is curly and beautiful,
In sea water it will rot.

The words of my brothers
Are those that have betrayed me.
The words of my brothers
Are those that have betrayed me.

Mother's words
Came true.
Mother's words
Came true.

Notes

Other version

Mamma mia dammi 100 lire
che in America voglio andà,
cento lire e le scarpette
ma in America no no no.

Suoi fratelli alla finestra
mamma mia lassela andà,
vai vai pure o figlia ingrata
che qualcosa succederà.

Quando furono in mezzo al mare
il bastimento si sprofondò,
pescator che peschi i pesci
la mia figlia vai tu a pescar.

Il mio sangue è rosso e fino
i pesci del mare lo beveran,
la mia carne è bianca e pura
la balena la mangerà.

Il consiglio della mia mamma
l'era tutta la verità,
mentre quello dei miei fratelli
resta quello che m'ha ingannà

Translation

Oh Mom, give me a hundred pounds
I want to go to America,
One hundred pounds and shoes,
But to America, no no no.

Her brothers at the window
Mom, let her go,
Go, go ahead, oh ungrateful daughter,
Something will happen.

When they were out at sea,
The vessel sank,
Fisherman who catch the fish,
Go fishing for my daughter.

My blood is red and fine,
The sea's fish will drink it,
My flesh is white and pure,
The whale will eat it.

The advice of my mother
Was the whole truth,
While that of my brothers
Is the one that betrayed me.

Here you can hear another version of this song on youtube
(http://www.youtube.com/watch?v=tT7frz7KFgo&feature=player_embedded).
You can watch a video of the 2nd version of the song as sung by Gigliola Cinquetti
(http://www.youtube.com/watch?v=mh2hfU5rl24).

For more about Mamma mia, dammi cento lire, go to:
http://www.mamalisa.com/?t=es&p=2598.

There, you'll find sheet music, a MIDI melody and a video performance.

38

Mano, mano morta (Hand, Dead Hand)

"Mano, mano morta" (Hand, Dead Hand) can also be found with the variation, "Mano, mano molle" (Hand, Limp Hand).

Mano, mano morta
(Italian Rhyme)

Mano, mano morta,
Dio la conforta,

Di pan' e di vino,
Tira un schiaffino.

Hand, Dead Hand
(English Translation)

Hand, dead hand,
God comforts it
With bread and with wine.
It gives a little slap.

Comments

Here are some other versions:

Lucia Bini wrote…

"My parents come from Friuli and I learnt this one:

*Mano mano morta
che batte sulla porta
Buum! (repeat several times at different tempos!)*

English translation

*Dead, dead hand
That hits upon the door,
Boom!*

*Dad would sit me on his lap and shake my floppy hand and then tap me on the
forehead with it at the buum! The idea of course is to fight being hit by your own
hand so it was an enjoyable game."*

*****

Rosa wrote, "I come from Calabria and I remember:

*Mano mano morta
Dio che ti comporta
Un pezzetino di pane
Un poccatino di vino
peri tup etti n'to mussino!*

English translation

*Dead hand hand,
God holds you up.
A little piece of bread
A little bit of wine
(Made up word) Peri tupetti on the little mouth!*

(As you make the child's hand give himself a little tap on the mouth.)"

*****

Here's a Sicilian version:

Manu modda manu modda
lu Signuri ti la 'ncodda
ti la 'ncodda cu la codda
manu modda manu modda

English translation

Limp hand, limp hand,
The Lord glues it for you.
He glues it with glue,
Limp hand, limp hand.

*****

Here's a Venetian version:

Man morta, man morta
pele de oca
pele de agnelo
daghe 'na sciafa a to fradelo,
to fradelo non ghe xè,
daghe 'na sciafa a chi ghe xè.

English translation

Dead hand, dead hand,
Goose skin,
Lamb skin,
Give a slap to your brother,
Your brother is not there
Give a slap to whoever is there.

For more about Mano, mano morta, go to:
http://www.mamalisa.com/?t=es&p=3340.

Maramao

"Maramao" is a cat. In some versions of the song he represents the Carnival (http://www.mamalisa.com/blog/carnival-in-italy-2/). The rhyme is recited on Shrove Tuesday, during the funeral of the Carnival, while the figure is being carried in its coffin to be burnt.

Maramao
(Italian Nursery Rhyme)

Fra' Maramao, perché sei morto?
Pan e vin non ti mancava,
l'insalata era nell'orto
e una casa avevi tu!
Maramao, perché sei morto?

Maramao
(English Translation)

Maramao, why are you dead?
You had salad in the garden,
And a home, and wine and bread!
Maramao - I beg your pardon -
Maramao, why are you dead?

For more about Maramao, go to: http://www.mamalisa.com/?t=es&p=887.

Maria lavava (Mary Busy with the Washing)

This selection is from Tuscany, but is well known elsewhere. It's used both as a lullaby and as a song or poem for children.

Maria lavava
(Italian Nursery Rhyme)

Maria lavava,
Giuseppe stendeva,
Il figlio piangeva
dal freddo che aveva.

Stai zitto mio figlio,
che adesso ti piglio:
il latte t'ho dato,
il pane non c'è.

La neve sui monti
cadeva dal cielo,
Maria col suo velo
copriva Gesù.

Mary Busy with the Washing
(English Translation)

Mary busy with the washing,
Joseph hung it out for drying,
All alone the baby lying
From the bitter cold was crying.

Hush my son, my little one,
In a moment I'll have done,
All my milk I've given to you
And the bread is finished, too.

As snow from the heavens
Fell over the mountains,
With her mantle of blue
Mary covered Jesu.

For more about Maria lavava, go to: http://www.mamalisa.com/?t=es&p=883.

41

Micio Miagolio (Kitty Cat)

My grandmother Maria used to sing this nursery song to my children. She learned it as a child from her parents, who immigrated to the U.S. from the Napoli area of Italy, in the early 20th century. This recording was done in June 2004 when she was 91 years old.

My grandmother spoke Italian, but never learned to write it, so the Italian is transliterated. People graciously wrote to me with what they think is the correct spelling, and I posted their responses below the rhyme.

Micio Miagolio
(Italian Dialect Children's Song)

Micio Miagolio
Vata Vatille
Che Te Mangiare

O Pane e casa
Nu mina Rata
Nu pugalia a mia
Frusti, frusti, frusti!

Kitty Cat
(English Translation)

Kitty Cat
Pussy Cat
What did you eat?
Bread and cheese
You didn't give me any
Not even a little bit
Hit, hit, hit!

Notes

Maria wrote from Italy:

"Hello,

*By chance I came across your interesting site where you say that your
grandmother used to sing the old Neapolitan nursery song MICIO MIAGOLIO to
your children.*

*I've read that you are looking for the correct spelling of this song in the
Neapolitan dialect and then I want to suggest some changes as I think that this
nursery rhyme should be written as follows:"*

*Musce muscille
Iatte iattille
Ch'ai da mangià
Pane e case
Nu me n'hai date
nu poculillo a me*

Fruste,fruste, fruste!

"Best regards from Italy.

Maria"

*****

*Nicoletta DeJoseph wrote me in October 2005 in response to my question about
the spelling of this rhyme:*

*"I had so much fun reading all the old Italian rhymes I grew up with in Italy. Now
me and my mom have so much fun singing these songs to my brother's kids. My*

dialect writing skills are not as good as my speech, but I think it goes like this:"

Micia Micella
Vatta Vattella
che t'a mangiato
O' pane e o' caso
nun mena dato nu poco a me
frusta la', frusta la', frusta la'

Nicoletta DeJoseph
Napoli

*****
JoyceAnna DiSclafani wrote me in June 2004, "What you have written, looks like a dialect which as you well know, is difficult to write out. Here it is in Italian:"

Micio Miagolo
Gatto Gattino
Che mangi tu?
Pane e cacio
Non me ne hai dato
Non prendere il mio
Frusti, frusti, frusti!

Game Instructions

Rub the cheeks on each line. Then on the last line, tap the cheeks.

For more about Micio Miagolio, go to: http://www.mamalisa.com/?t=es&p=898.

There, you'll find an MP3 tune.

42

Mie Mama Mata Mata (Coo-roo, Coo-roo)

Mie Mama Mata Mata
(Italian Dialect Nursery Rhyme)

Mie mama mata mata
la m'ha mis dentar in t'la pignata.
Mia surela bela bela
l'ha m'ha mis in t'la ziztela.
Mie popà luin luon
al m'ha magnà tutt'in tun con.
Par l'amor ad San Martin
son d'vantà un bel uslin:
cirolo cirolo cirolo!

Coo-roo, Coo-roo
(English Translation)

Coo-roo, coo-roo, my dotty mam
Stuffed me in the stewing pan.
My fair sister, scamper scamper,
Packed me in the picnic hamper.
Then my dada for his lunch
Wolfed me down in one big munch.
By the holy saints above,
I became a milk-white dove.
This is my song, coo-roo, coo-roo,
This is the song I sing for you!

Comments

Standard Italian Translation
La mia mamma, matta matta

La mia mamma, matta matta
M'ha pigiato nella pignatta.
Mia sorella, bella bella
M'ha posato nel cestello.
Il mio papà, quatton quattoni
M'ha pappato in un boccone.

Per l'amor di San Martino
Son diventato un bel uccellino:
Cip, cip, cip!

Note on dialect:

In t'la ziztela= nel cestino
tutt'in tun con= tutto in un boccone
son d'vantà = sono diventato

For more about Mie Mama Mata Mata, go to:
http://www.mamalisa.com/?t=es&p=884.

43

Milano Torino (Milan Turin)

Anna wrote, "This song was used to decide which child would go first."

Milano Torino
(Italian Counting-out Song)

Milano Torino è una bella città
Si dorme, si beve e l'amore si fa.
Ai visto mio marito ?
Si!
Che colore era vestito ?
Rosso!
Se il rosso è su di te
Conta uno due tre,
Uno due tre.

Milan Turin
(English Translation)

Milan, Turin, is a beautiful town,
They sleep, they drink, and they make love.
"Have you seen my husband?"
"Yes!"
"What color was he wearing?"
"Red!"
"If red is on you,
Count one, two, three."
"One, two, three."

For more about Milano Torino, go to: http://www.mamalisa.com/?t=es&p=2218.

44

Nanna cunetta (As You're Sleeping in Your Bed)

Nanna cunetta
(Italian Children's Song)

Nanna cunetta
Mamma è andata a messa
Papà è andato in campi
Con tre cavalli bianchi.

As You're Sleeping in Your Bed
(English Translation)

As you're sleeping in your bed,
Mama has gone to church.
Papa has gone to work in the fields,
With three white horses.

Notes

At the end you make a clicking sound with your tongue on the roof of your mouth to sound like the clicking of horses' hooves.

For more about Nanna cunetta, go to: http://www.mamalisa.com/?t=es&p=873.

45

Nella vecchia fattoria (On the Old Farm)

This is "Old McDonald Had a Farm" in Italian...

Nella vecchia fattoria
(Italian Children's Song)

Nella vecchia fattoria,
ia-ia-o
Quante bestie ha zio Tobia,
ia-ia-o
C'e il cane (bau!) cane (bau!) ca-ca-cane, cane (bau!)
Quante bestie ha zio Tobia,
ia-ia-o

Nella vecchia fattoria,
ia-ia-o
Quante bestie ha zio Tobia,
ia-ia-o
E il gatto (miao!) gatto (miao!) ga-ga-gatto, gatto (miao!)
Quante bestie ha zio Tobia,
ia-ia-o

Nella vecchia fattoria,
ia-ia-o
Quante bestie ha zio Tobia,
ia-ia-o
E la muca (muu!) muca (muu!) mu-mu-muca, muca (muu!)
Quante bestie ha zio Tobia,
ia-ia-o

On the Old Farm
(English Translation)

On the old farm,
E ah e ah o!
What a lot of animals Uncle Tobias has,
E ah e ah o!
There's the dog, bow! Dog, bow! D-d-dog,
What a lot of animals Uncle Tobias has,
E ah e ah o!

On the old farm,
E ah e ah o!
What a lot of animals Uncle Tobias has,
E ah e ah o!
There's the cat, meow! Cat, meow! C-c-cat,
What a lot of animals Uncle Tobias has,
E ah e ah o!

On the old farm,
E ah e ah o!
What a lot of animals Uncle Tobias has,
E ah e ah o!
There's the cow, mooo! Cow, mooo! C-c-cow,
What a lot of animals Uncle Tobias has,
E ah e ah o!

Comments

Victoria wrote "This is 'Old McDonald Had a Farm' in Italian, I learned it this year in my Italian class".

Kelly wrote: "I found your website while I was searching for Italian lullabies and nursery rhymes. I would like to learn some to teach to my daughter, who is 2 months old. I learned OLD MACDONALD *in my Italian class last fall:*

Nella vecchia fattoria
i-a i-a o!
Quante bestia h'zio Tobia
i-a i-a o!
C'e un cane bau! cane bau! ca-ca-cane
e un gatto miao! gatto miao! ga-ga-gatto
e la mucca muuu! mucca muuu! mu-mu-mucca
Nella vecchia fattoria
i-a i-a o!

ENGLISH TRANSLATION

On the old farm,
E ah e ah o!
What a lot of animals Uncle Tobias has,
E ah e ah o!
There's a dog, bow! Dog, bow! D-d-dog
And a cat, meow! Cat, meow! C-c-cat
And the cow, mooo! Cow, mooo! C-c-cow,
On the old farm,
E ah e ah o!

For more about Nella vecchia fattoria, go to:
http://www.mamalisa.com/?t=es&p=877.

There, you'll find a video performance.

46

Ninna nanna a sette e venti (Lullaby At Twenty Past Seven)

Ninna nanna a sette e venti
(Italian Lullaby)

Ninna nanna a sette e venti,
il bambino s'addormenti.
s'addormenta e fa un bel sonno
e si sveglia domani a giorno.
Nanna ieri, nanna ieri
e le sporte non son panieri
e i panieri non son le sporte
e la vita non è la morte
e la morte non è la vita.
La canzone l'è già finita.

Lullaby At Twenty Past Seven
(English Translation)

Lullaby at twenty past seven,
The child falls asleep,
Falls asleep and has a good sleep,
And wakes up tomorrow at day-break.
Lullaby yesterday, lullaby yesterday,
Shopping bags are not baskets,
And baskets are not shopping bags,
Life is not death,
And death is not life.
The song is already finished.

For more about Ninna nanna a sette e venti, go to:
http://www.mamalisa.com/?t=es&p=2195.

Therc, you'll find an MP3 tune.

Ninnananna di Fra' Simon (Brother Simon's Lullaby)

Ninnananna di Fra' Simon
(Italian Lullaby)

Din don Din don,
la campana di fra' Simon,
eran due che la sonavan,
pane vin i' domandavan.

Din don campanon.
La campana di fra' Simon la sonava nott'e dì:
che il giorno l'è finì ed è ora di dormir.
Din don Din don.

Brother Simon's Lullaby
(English Translation)

Ding-dong, ding-dong,
Brother Simon's bell,
Two men were playing it,
Asking for bread and wine.

Ding-dong, big bell.
Brother Simon used to play the bell night and day;
The day is over and it's sleeping time.
Ding-dong, ding-dong.

For more about Ninnananna di Fra' Simon, go to:
http://www.mamalisa.com/?t=es&p=882.

There, you'll find sheet music and an MP3 tune.

48

Ninnananna di Gesù Bambino (Infant Jesus' Lullaby)

Ninnananna di Gesù Bambino
(Italian Lullaby)

Gesù Bambino è nato,
è nato in Betlem;
è sopra un po' di paglia,
è sopra un po' di fien.
E' sopra un po' di fien.
Gesù Bambino piange,
la mamma che lo adora,
è sopra un po' di fien.

Infant Jesus' Lullaby
(English Translation)

Infant Jesus is born,
is born in Bethlehem;
He's lying on straw,
He's lying on hay.
He's lying on hay.
Infant Jesus is crying,
His mother is adoring him,
He's lying on hay.

For more about Ninnananna di Gesù Bambino, go to:
http://www.mamalisa.com/?t=es&p=878.

There, you'll find sheet music, an MP3 tune and a MIDI melody.

Ninna nanna, ninna oh (Lullaby, Lullaby, ooh)

Ninna nanna, ninna oh
(Italian Lullaby)

Ninna nanna, ninna oh
Questo bimbo a chi lo dò ?
Se lo dò alla Befana,
Se lo tiene una settimana.
Se lo dò all'uomo nero,
Se lo tiene un anno intero.
Ninna nanna, ninna oh,
Questo bimbo me lo terrò!

Lullaby, Lullaby, ooh
(English Translation)

Lullaby, lullaby, ooh,
Who will I give this baby to?
If I give him to the old hag,
For a week she will keep him, ahh.
If I give him to the bogeyman,
For a whole year he'll keep him,
Lullaby, lullaby, eeee
I will keep this baby for me!

Notes

"La Befana" is translated here as "old hag". "La Befana" is also a name for the old lady who brings gifts to children around Christmastime in parts of Italy. As that figure, "La Befana" represents the Epiphany (celebrated on January 6th), which is when the 3 magi brought gifts to Jesus. Some children are brought gifts on the eve of the Epiphany by "La Befana". We're not certain, but we believe that in this song "La Befana" does not refer to that figure, but rather to a more general "old hag". You can read more about "La Befana" here (http://www.mamalisa.com/blog/in-italy-on-january-6th-befana-comes-with-gift-for-kids-for-the-epiphany/).

"L'uomo nero" is the bogeyman. In Italian, the phrase literally translates to "black man" because he's dressed in a long black coat with a hood hiding his face.

("Black man" has no rascist connotations.) "L'uomo nero" doesn't usually harm kids, but he does take them away to a scary place. In this lullaby, he takes them away for a year.

I asked Emanuela Marsura, an Italian teacher, about the "l'uomo nero" (black man). Here's what she wrote:

"Our 'black man' (l'uomo nero) is a character of fantasy that every mother and father mentions to his child to persuade him he has to go to sleep or eat without a tantrum. We also have a game about 'l'uomo nero' (http://mamalisa.com/?t=es&p=3346&c=120).

Every child imagines the black-man in a different way, but certainly scary, dark. Mom and Dad say that the black man can take away the children."

*****

Toni MacNeish sent us another version of this lullaby:

Ninna nanna, ninna oh
Questo bimbo a chi lo do?
Se lo do alla befana
Se lo tiene una settimana
Se lo do al lupo nero
Se lo tiene un anno intero
Se lo do a lupo bianco
Se lo tiene tanto tanto
Ninna oh ninna oh
A nessuno lo darò!

Translation

Lullaby, lullaby, ooh.
Who will I give this baby to?
If I give him to the old hag
For a week she will keep him.
If I give him to the black wolf
For a whole year he'll keep him
If I give him to the white wolf
For very long he'll keep him,
Lullaby, lullaby, lullaby, hmm
To no one I'll give him!

Comments

For more about Ninna nanna, ninna oh, go to:
http://www.mamalisa.com/?t=es&p=2168.

There, you'll find sheet music and a MIDI melody.

50

Oh che bel castello (Oh, What a Fine Castle)

Oh che bel castello
(Italian Circle Game Song)

"Oh che bel castello
marcondirondirondello,
oh che bel castello
marcondirondirondà."

"Il mio è ancora più bello
marcondirondirondello,

il mio è ancora più bello
marcondirondirondà."

"E noi lo ruberemo
marcondirondirondello,
e noi lo ruberemo
marcondirondirondà."

"E noi lo rifaremo
marcondirondirondello,
e noi lo rifaremo
marcondirondirondà."

"E noi lo bruceremo
marcondirondirondello,
e noi lo bruceremo
marcondirondirondà."

"E noi lo spegneremo
marcondirondirondello,
e noi lo spegneremo
marcondirondirondà."

Oh, What a Fine Castle
(English Translation)

"Oh, what a fine castle,
marcon-diron-dirondello,
Oh, what a fine castle,
marcon-diron-dironda."

"Mine is much finer,
marcon-diron-dirondello,
Mine is much finer,
marcon-diron-dironda."

"We will steal it,
marcon-diron-dirondello,
We will steal it,
marcon-diron-dironda."

"We'll build it again,
marcon-diron-dirondello,
We'll build it again,
marcon-diron-dironda."

"We will scorch it,
marcon-diron-dirondello,
We will scorch it,
marcon-diron-dironda."

"We'll put the fire out,

marcon-diron-dirondello,
We'll put the fire out,
marcon-diron-dironda."

Notes

Here's an alternate version for the 3rd through 6th verses in the original Italian, followed by an English translation:

E noi lo distruggeremo,
marcondirondirondello,
E noi lo distruggeremo,
marcondirondironda.

E come farete,
marcondirondirondello,
E come farete,
marcondirondironda.

Togliendo una pietra,
marcondirondirondello,
Togliendo una pietra,
marcondirondironda.

E chi è questa pietra,
marcondirondirondello,
E chi è questa pietra,
marcondirondironda.

Questa pietra è (...),
marcondirondirondello,
Questa pietra è (...),
marcondirondironda.

English Translation

We will destroy it,
marcondirondirondello,
We will destroy it,
marcondirondironda.

How will you do it?
marcondirondirondello,
How will you do it?
marcondirondironda.

We'll take a stone out,
marcondirondirondello,
We'll take a stone out,
marcondirondironda.

And who is this stone?

marcondirondirondello,
And who is this stone?
marcondirondironda.

This stone is (child's name),
marcondirondirondello,
This stone is (child's name),
marcondirondironda.

Game Instructions

The children stand in two circles. The first circle should have two children, the second should have all the other kids. The kids in both circles start going around in a circle while singing the song. When they reach the last verse, the children in the first circle say the name of a child in the second circle who then joins them and so on till there are only two children left in the second circle.

Then the game can start again from the beginning.

For more about Oh che bel castello, go to:
http://www.mamalisa.com/?t=es&p=3334.

There, you'll find a video performance.

51

Oh veni, sonnu (Oh Come Sleep)

This song is in the Sicilian dialect.

Oh veni, sonnu
(Sicilian Dialect Lullaby)

Oh, veni, sonnu, di la muntanedda.
Lu lupu si mangiau la picuredda.
Oi ninì
ninna vò fa.

Oh, veni, sonnu, di la landa mia.
Lu me figghiolu muta mi vurria.
Oi ninì
ninna vò fa.

Oh Come Sleep
(English Translation)

Oh come, sleep, from the little mountain.
The wolf devoured the little sheep.
Oh, child
wants to sleep.

Oh come, sleep, from my heath.
My little son would want me to be quiet*.
Oh, child
wants to sleep.

Notes

*Gian Carlo originally translated this line as, "My little son would want me mute".
I asked him about this line since "mute" sounds harsh in English. "Mute" is used to
describe someone who isn't ABLE to talk... not normally to say that you don't
WANT someone to talk. "My little son would want me to be quiet" or "My little son
would want me to hush" would sound more natural in English.*

Gian Carlo wrote back, "...these changes are okay. As a matter of fact, in Italian "muto" ("muta" is the feminine) is also not used to describe that you don't want someone to talk. It sounds "strong" in a lullaby. But you know: lullabies are strange, and here, probably, the metrics sounded better using a short word instead of a longer word corresponding to quiet or hush: like 'silenziosa'."

******

Standard Italian translation

Oh, vieni, sonno, dalla montagnola.
Il lupo si mangiò la pecorella.
Oh, il bambino,
vuol fare la nanna.

Oh vieni, sonno, dalla landa mia.
Il mio figliolo muta mi vorrebbe.
Oh, il bambino,
vuol fare la nanna.

Comments

*****

This is the version from Bagnara Calabra

Oh veni, sonnu, di la muntanella.
Lu lupu si mangiau la picurella.
Oh, mammà,
la ninna vò fa.

Oh veni, sonnu, di la landa mia.
Lu me figghiolu muta mi vurria.
Oh, mammà,
la ninna vò fa.

Standard Italian translation

Oh vieni, sonno, dalla montagnola.
Il lupo si mangiò la pecorella.
Oh, mamma,
(il bambino) vuol fare la nanna.

Oh vieni, sonno, dalla landa mia.
Il mio figliolo muta mi vorrebbe.
Oh, mamma,
(il bambino) vuol fare la nanna.

English translation

Oh come, sleep, from the little mountain.
The wolf devoured the little sheep.
Oh, mama,

(child) wants to sleep.

Oh come, sleep, from my heath.
My little son could want me mute.
Oh, mama,
(child) wants to sleep.

For more about Oh veni, sonnu, go to: http://www.mamalisa.com/?t=es&p=2198.

There, you'll find an MP3 tune.

52

Peppina prendi un pettine (Peppina, Get a Comb)

Peppina prendi un pettine
(Italian Tongue Twister)

Peppina prendi un pettine.
E pettinami un po'.
Un po' Peppina pettina.
Ma poi si impappinò.
Peppina aspetta un pettine
Per pettinarmi un po'.

Peppina, Get a Comb
(English Translation)

Peppina, get a comb
and comb my hair a little.
Peppina combs a little,
But then became confused.
Peppina waits for a comb
in order to comb my hair a little.

Notes

"Now I understand this tongue twister - when I see how long it takes my daughter to comb her hair, I finally understand the line about her becoming confused about combing hair! lol" -Mama Lisa

For more about Peppina prendi un pettine , go to:
http://www.mamalisa.com/?t=es&p=3332.

53

Personent hodie (This Day Resounds)

Personent hodie is a Latin carol from 1582.

Personent hodie
(Latin Christmas Carol)

Personent hodie
voces puerulae,
laudantes iucunde
qui nobis est natus,
summo Deo datus,
et de virgineo ventre procreatus.

In mundo nascitur,
pannis involvitur
praesepi ponitur
stabulo brutorum,
rector supernorum.
perdidit spolia princeps infernorum.

Magi tres venerunt,
parvulum inquirunt,
Bethlehem adeunt,
stellulam sequendo,
ipsum adorando,
aurum, thus, et myrrham ei offerendo.

Omnes clericuli,
pariter pueri,
cantent ut angeli:
advenisti mundo,
laudes tibi fundo.
ideo gloria in excelsis Deo.

This Day Resounds
(English Translation)

This day resounds
With the voices of children
Pleasantly praising

He who was born and given to us,
The Lord most high
Born of the Virgin womb.

Born in the world,
Wrapped in swaddling garments
Placed in the manger,
In the stall of beasts
Lord of above
Destroyed the spoils of the prince of hell.

The three Magi came
In search of a little child,
They go to Bethlehem
Following the little stars
Worshiping him,
Offering him gold, frankincense and myrrh.

All the clergy,
Children as well
Sing like the angels:
You come to the world
Praise to thee.
Glory to God in the Highest.

Notes

The translation above is more literal than the one below, which is a well-known English translation by Jane M. Joseph (1894–1929).

On This Day Earth Shall Ring

On this day earth shall ring
with the song children sing
to the Lord, Christ our King,
born on earth to save us;
him the Father gave us.
Refrain
Id-e-o-o-o, id-e-o-o-o,
Id-e-o gloria in excelsis Deo!

His the doom, ours the mirth;
when he came down to earth,
Bethlehem saw his birth;
ox and ass beside him
from the cold would hide him.
Refrain

God's bright star, o'er his head,
Wise Men three to him led;
kneel they low by his bed,
lay their gifts before him,

praise him and adore him.
Refrain

On this day angels sing;
with their song earth shall ring,
praising Christ, heaven's King,
born on earth to save us;
peace and love he gave us.
Refrain

Photos & Illustrations

Comments

The image is of Personent hodie from the 1582 edition of Piae Cantiones.

For more about Personent hodie, go to: http://www.mamalisa.com/?t=es&p=3320.

There, you'll find an MP3 tune.

54

Piazza bella piazza (Plaza, Pretty Plaza)

Piazza bella piazza
(Italian Finger Play)

Piazza bella piazza,
Ci passò una lepre pazza:
Il Pollice la vide;
L'Indice le sparò;
Il Medio la scuoiò
L'Anulare la cucinò
E il Mignolino se la mangiò.

Plaza, Pretty Plaza
(English Translation)

Plaza, pretty plaza,
There passed a mad hare:
Thumb saw it,
Pointer shot it,
Middle-finger skinned it,
Ring-finger cooked it
And Little Pinkie ate it.

For more about Piazza bella piazza, go to:
http://www.mamalisa.com/?t=es&p=3325.

55

Piva piva l'oli d'uliva (Piva, Piva, Olive Oil)

Gian Carlo wrote: "Here is a Christmas carol that's very famous in Lombardy (I'm sure, there are other versions from other regions of Italy). In Lombardy there are different versions; below is the version most sung here where I live, between Milan and Bergamo.

'Piva' and 'baghet' indicates both a sort of bagpipe. When I was a child, a band had formed with a lot of 'birlifù' ('birlifù' is a sort of panflute) of different sizes, one 'piva', one fife, and one bass drum (called 'tamburù', i.e. big drum). They rehearsed near my home and I often went and listen to those wonderful Christmas carols.

This song is so famous that Christmas carols are also called "pive" in Lombardy."

Piva piva l'oli d'uliva
(Italian Dialect Christmas Carol)

Piva piva l'oli d'uliva,
piva piva l'oli d'ulà.*
'L è 'l Bambin che porta i belé
l'è la mama che spènd i dané.

Piva piva l'oli d'uliva,
gnaca gnaca l'oli che taca.**
'L è 'l Bambin che porta i belé
l'è la mama che spènd i dané.

Piva piva suna la piva,
piva piva suna 'l baghèt.
Canta, canta bèla fiùr:
'l è nasìt ol nòst Signùr

Gh'è gnà fassa, gnà panisèl
per fassà chèl Bambì bèl.
Gh'è gnà fassa, gnà lensöl
per fasà chèl bèl Fiöl.

Piva, Piva, Olive Oil
(English Translation)

Piva, piva, olive oil,
Piva, piva, "ula" oil.*
It's the Child who brings the presents,
It's (your) mother who spends money.

Piva, piva, olive oil,
Gnaca, gnaca, sticky oil.**
It's the Child who brings the presents,
It's (your) mother who spends money.

Piva, piva, the bagpipe sounds,
Piva, piva, the bagpipe sounds.
Sing, sing, beautiful flower:
Our Lord is born.

There are no swaddling bands of cloth,
There are no clothes to swaddle that beautiful Child.
There are no swaddling bands of cloth,
There are no sheets to swaddle that beautiful Child.

Notes

*Gian Carlo wrote, "I don't know if "piva piva" at the beginning of some verses
has to be translated, since it seems to have only a 'musical' purpose. Also 'oli
d'uliva' (olive oil) and 'oli d'ulà' ('ulà oil' – 'ulà' is a non-existent word) have only
a musical purpose."*

**Gian Carlo wrote, "The second verse in this version sounds like nonsense, since I don't know what 'gnaca' could mean. 'Taca' is a verb that in northern dialects can have different meanings, i.e.: to hang up something, to paste something on a wall, to begin, to catch to a bottom of a pan (with reference to a food), to be sticky."*

Regarding "swaddling bands of cloth" - this refers to a cloth tied together with thinner strips of cloth to swaddle the baby Jesus. It's referred to in the Bible.

Photos & Illustrations

Comments

Gian Carlo sent us the photos on this page with this note: "Enclosed you can find some photos about Santa Lucia celebration here in Lombardy (http://www.mamalisa.com/blog/the-celebration-of-santa-lucia-in-italy/). Now I can also show you the 'baghèt' (that I cited when I sent the Piva Piva carol): a little bagpipe, as you can see. I took all photos in Arzago d'Adda (Lombardy, about 30 km from Bergamo and 30 km from Milan)."

For more about Piva piva l'oli d'uliva, go to:
http://www.mamalisa.com/?t=es&p=2217.

There, you'll find a video performance.

Prezzemolo in mezzo (Parsley Put Itself in the Middle)

Prezzemolo in mezzo
(Italian Children's Song)

Prezzemolo nel mezzo si ficcò,
la casa crollò,
prezzemolo in mezzo si trovò.

Parsley Put Itself in the Middle
(English Translation)

Parsley put itself in the middle,
The house collapsed,
And parsley found itself in the middle.

For more about Prezzemolo in mezzo, go to:
http://www.mamalisa.com/?t=es&p=2770.

57

Questo l'occhio bello (This One, The Beautiful Eye)

Questo l'occhio bello
(Italian Finger Play)

Questo l'occhio bello
Questo suo fratello
Questa la chiesina
Questa la campanilina
din din din.

This One, The Beautiful Eye
(English Translation)

This one, the beautiful eye,
This one, its brother,
This one, the little church,

This one, the tiny little bell,
Din, din, din.

Game Instructions

Point to one eye
Point to the other
Point to the mouth
Point to the nose
Hold nose and move from side to side.

For more about Questo l'occhio bello, go to:
http://www.mamalisa.com/?t=es&p=881.

58

San Nicolò de Bari (Saint Nicholas of Bari)

Here's a St. Nicholas Day rhyme from Veneto.

Saint Nicholas Day is celebrated on December 6th in the north-east of Italy, mainly in the region that belonged to the Austro-Hungarian Empire. St. Nick is the one who brings children presents in that area, instead of Santa, Father Christmas or La Befana (http://www.mamalisa.com/blog/in-italy-on-january-6th-befana-comes-with-gift-for-kids-for-the-epiphany/).

San Nicolò de Bari
(Italian Dialect Saint Nicholas Day Rhyme)

San Nicolò de Bari
Le festa dei scolari
Se i scolari no vol far festa
San Nicolò ghe taia la testa.

Saint Nicholas of Bari
(English Translation)

Saint Nicholas of Bari,
The schoolchildren's celebration,
If the schoolchildren don't celebrate,
Saint Nicholas will chop their heads off.

Notes

Alternate last line: Ghe taieremo la testa (We'll chop their heads off.)

For more about San Nicolò de Bari , go to:
http://www.mamalisa.com/?t=es&p=3260.

There, you'll find a video performance.

59

Santa Lucia

This Santa Lucia song is about a section in Naples. It's tune has been adapted for use in some Scandinavian songs that are sung for the holiday of Santa Lucia.

Santa Lucia
(Italian Santa Lucia Song)

Sul mare luccica l'astro d'argento.
Placida è l'onda, prospero è il vento.
Sul mare luccica l'astro d'argento.
Placida è l'onda, prospero è il vento.
Venite all'agile barchetta mia,
Santa Lucia! Santa Lucia!
Venite all'agile barchetta mia,
Santa Lucia! Santa Lucia!

Con questo zeffiro, così soave,
Oh, com'è bello star sulla nave!
Con questo zeffiro, così soave,
Oh, com'è bello star sulla nave!
Su passegieri, venite via!
Santa Lucia! Santa Lucia!
Su passegieri, venite via!
Santa Lucia! Santa Lucia!

In fra le tende, bandir la cena
In una sera così serena,
In fra le tende, bandir la cena
In una sera così serena,
Chi non dimanda, chi non desia.
Santa Lucia! Santa Lucia!
Chi non dimanda, chi non desia.
Santa Lucia! Santa Lucia!

Mare sì placida, vento sì caro,
Scordar fa i triboli al marinaro,
Mare sì placida, vento sì caro,
Scordar fa i triboli al marinaro,
E va gridando con allegria,
Santa Lucia! Santa Lucia!
E va gridando con allegria,
Santa Lucia! Santa Lucia!

O dolce Napoli, o suol beato,
Ove sorridere volle il creato,
O dolce Napoli, o suol beato,
Ove sorridere volle il creato,
Tu sei l'impero dell'armonia,
Santa Lucia! Santa Lucia!
Tu sei l'impero dell'armonia,
Santa Lucia! Santa Lucia!

Or che tardate? Bella è la sera.
Spira un'auretta fresca e leggiera.
Or che tardate? Bella è la sera.
Spira un'auretta fresca e leggiera.
Venite all'agile barchetta mia,
Santa Lucia! Santa Lucia!
Venite all'agile barchetta mia,
Santa Lucia! Santa Lucia!

Santa Lucia
(English Translation)

The silver star shimmers on the sea,
The wave is peaceful, the wind is favorable.
The silver star shimmers on the sea,
The wave is peaceful, the wind is favorable.

Come to my sprightly little boat,
Santa Lucia, Santa Lucia!
Come to my sprightly little boat,
Santa Lucia, Santa Lucia!

With this breeze so sweet,
Oh, how lovely it is to be on a boat!
With this breeze so sweet,
Oh, how lovely it is to be on a boat!
Come on passengers, come away!
Santa Lucia, Santa Lucia!
Come on passengers, come away!
Santa Lucia, Santa Lucia!

Amid the sails, supper is ready
On this night so serene.
Amid the sails, supper is ready
On this night so serene,
With no demands, with no desires,
Santa Lucia, Santa Lucia!
With no demands, with no desires,
Santa Lucia, Santa Lucia!

This sea so calm, this wind so dear,
Makes the sailor forget his troubles.
This sea so calm, this wind so dear,
Makes the sailor forget his troubles.
And he is shouting cheerfully,
Santa Lucia, Santa Lucia!
And he is shouting cheerfully,
Santa Lucia, Santa Lucia!

Oh sweet Naples, oh blessed land,
Where Creation wished to smile!
Oh sweet Naples, oh blessed land,
Where Creation wished to smile!
You are the realm of harmony,
Santa Lucia, Santa Lucia!
You are the realm of harmony,
Santa Lucia, Santa Lucia!

Now why delay? The night is beautiful,
A cool and light breeze is blowing.
Now why delay? The night is beautiful,
A cool and light breeze is blowing.
Come to my sprightly little boat,
Santa Lucia, Santa Lucia!
Come to my sprightly little boat,
Santa Lucia, Santa Lucia!

Notes

I asked Gian Carlo in Italy about this song and he wrote: "The only famous Italian song I remember about Santa Lucia has the same tune as the one people sing in Sweden (http://www.mamalisa.com/?t=es&p=1302&c=86). The Santa Lucia song (a barcarolla) is the first song ever translated from Neapolitan into Italian. In this song, however, Santa Lucia is the historical quarter of Naples."

FYI "A barcarolla" refers to the style of music sung by the gondoliers of Venice.

*****

Here's a non-literal but singable English translation by Maria X. Hayes from the early 1900's:

1.
Now 'neath the silver moon
Ocean is glowing,
O'er the calm billow
Soft winds are blowing.
Now 'neath the silver moon
Ocean is glowing,
O'er the calm billow
Soft winds are blowing.

Here balmy breezes* blow,
Pure joys invite us,
And as we gently row,
All things delight us.
Here balmy breezes blow,
Pure joys invite us,
And as we gently row,
All things delight us.

Who then will sail with me
In my bark o'er the sea?
Santa Lucia! Santa Lucia!
Who then will sail with me
In my bark o'er the sea?
Santa Lucia! Santa Lucia!

Who will embark with me
On yonder sparkling sea?
Santa Lucia, Santa Lucia!
Who will embark with me
On yonder sparkling sea?
Santa Lucia, Santa Lucia!

When o'er thy waters
Light winds are playing
Thy spell can sooth us
All care allaying
Hark, how the sailor's cry
Joyously echoes nigh:
Santa Lucia!

To thee, sweet Napoli,
What charms are given,
Where smiles creation,
Toil blest by heaven.
Home of fair Poesy,
Realm of pure Harmony,
Santa Lucia!

*Originally translated as "zephyrs".

Comments

"Santa Lucia" was transcribed by Teodoro Cottrau (1827–1879) in the original Neapolitan and published in 1849 in Naples. Later Cottrau translated it into standard Italian.

For more about Santa Lucia, go to: http://www.mamalisa.com/?t=es&p=3318.

There, you'll find a MIDI melody and a video performance.

60

Sedia, sediola (Chair, Little Chair)

Valentina wrote: "I am Roman, this is the only version I have always known of "Sedia, sediola" and it is in Italian..."

Sedia, sediola
(Italian Lap Rhyme)

Se-dia*
sedio-la
(Nome) va a scuo-la
si porta il ca-nestre-llo
pie-no pieno di pizzu-tello
la mae-stra
gli fa fe-sta
e glielo butta da-lla
finestra.

Chair, Little Chair
(English Translation)

Cha-air*
Little chair
(Kid's Name) goes to school
He brings a basket
Full, full of pizzutello (grapes)**
The teacher
Greets him
And pushes him through
The window.

Notes

The dash equals a pause stretching the vowel sound of the preceding syllable
**Pizzutello is a type of grapes which are a specialty of the town of Tivoli, near Rome.*

*****

Game Instructions

"You sing it by holding a child's hands while he or she is seated on your lap facing you, with legs apart. While singing you let him or her move his back to and fro; while pronouncing the last lines you let him go further from you (always holding his hands) as if pretending to let him fall out of a window, like the last lines of the song say. Children enjoy a little dose of scary excitement." -Valentina

For more about Sedia, sediola, go to: http://www.mamalisa.com/?t=es&p=3104.

There, you'll find a video performance.

61

Sega sega mastu Ciccio (Saw Saw, Master Ciccio)

This rhyme was popular in the Neapolitan region of Italy.

Sega sega mastu Ciccio
(Italian Dialect Nursery Rhyme)

Sega sega mastu Ciccio
na panèlla e nu sacìccio;
'o sasiccio ce 'o pappammo
e 'a panella ce 'a stipamme.

Saw Saw, Master Ciccio
(English Translation)

Saw saw, master Ciccio,
A little potato and a sausage
The sausage, we eat it
And the little potato, we keep it.

Notes

Here's the rhyme in standard Italian:

Sega sega mastro Ciccio
una patatina e una salsiccia
la salsiccia ce la mangiamo
e la patatina ce la conserviamo

***

Adriana sent this version:

The lyrics I know are these (in Neapolitan dialect), but there are slightly different versions in other parts of Southern Italy:

Sega, sega mastu Ciccio,

na panèlla e nu sasiccio;
'o sasiccio c' 'o mangiammo
e a panella c' 'a stipammo.
c' 'a stipàmmo pe' Natale,
quanno vènene 'e zampugnàre!

Translation:
Saw saw, master Ciccio (=Francesco),
A round loaf and a sausage
The sausage, we eat it
And the round loaf, we keep it.
We keep it for the Christmas period
when the pipers (=players of reed-pipe) arrive.

Game Instructions

Put the child on your lap. Hold his/her hands and gently move them back and forth like you're sawing.

Comments

Joann wrote: "My aunt was from Naples and always sang a song to our children. She was not sure what the English translation was. With the children on her lap she would push the back and pull them forward while singing the song. Since she spoke dialect I am not sure of the words but to our best knowledge the beginning line was "Sega, sega". Our family was delighted to hear the song from the 91 year old woman, Mici Miagolio (http://www.mamalisa.com/?t=es&p=898&c=120). That was another song that she sang to the children. Thanks for your website."

Salvatore wrote:

"Ciao, I remember this song clearly. My grandmother would sing this. When she got a package with string, she would make a triangle using both my fingers and hers, then pull the string through it making a seesaw like movement. she would then sing Sega, Sega. In fact, as kids, if we wanted to play with a string with our friends we would call it 'Sega Sega'."

-Salvatore Lenzi
Gemini Travel Agency, Inc. (http://www.geminitravelagency.com/)

Come join our discussion of Sega Sega Mastu Ciccio (http://www.mamalisa.com/blog/the-italian-song-sega-sega-mastro-ciccio-plus-someones-looking-for-the-lyrics-to-saga-saga-master-cheech/) on Mama Lisa's World Blog.

For more about Sega sega mastu Ciccio, go to:
http://www.mamalisa.com/?t=es&p=2843.

There, you'll find a video performance.

62

Se sei felice tu lo sai (If You're Happy and You Know It)

Se sei felice tu lo sai
(Italian Children's Song)

Se sei felice tu lo sai
batti le mani
Se sei felice tu lo sai
batti le mani
Se sei felice tu lo sai
e ridere potrai
Se sei felice tu lo sai
batti le mani.

If You're Happy and You Know It
(English Translation)

If you're happy and you know it
Clap your hands,
If you're happy and you know it
Clap your hands,
If you're happy and you know it
And you really want to show it,
If you're happy and you know it
Clap your hands.

For more about Se sei felice tu lo sai, go to:
http://www.mamalisa.com/?t=es&p=880.

There, you'll find a MIDI melody.

63

Seta moneta (Silk Money)

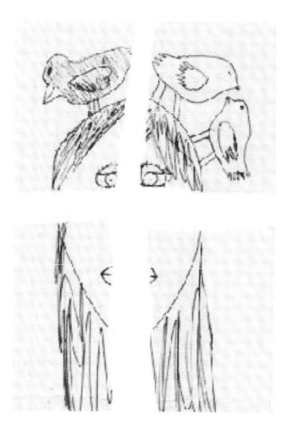

Emanuela wrote from Italy: "'Seta moneta' is a rhyme that is used to relax children when they are little. It's said in a tone of voice that gets lower and lower, while the children close their eyes and they fall asleep with the last whisper. It's a sweet lullaby."

Seta moneta
(Italian Lullaby)

Seta moneta
le donne di Gaeta
che filano la seta
la seta e la bambagia
bambini chi vi piace
ci piace Giovanni
che fa cantare i galli
la chioccia coi pulcini
i galli e le galline
che fanno coccodèè
canta gallina
fa l'ovo domattina
vicino al gallo rosso
vicino al gallo bianco
che fa chicchirichì

Seta moneta
le donne di Gaeta
che filano la seta
la filan troppo forte
e fan tremar le porte
le porte son d'argento
e fanno cinquecento
centocinquanta
tutto il mondo canta

Canta lo gallo
risponde la gallina
Madama Colombina
s'affaccia alla finestra
con tre colombe in testa
Passan tre fanti
su tre cavalli bianchi:
bianca la sella,
bianca la donzella,
bianco il parafieno
Seta moneta
le donne di Gaeta
che filano la seta
la seta e la bambagia....

....bambini vi è piaciuta?

Silk Money
(English Translation)

Silk, money,
Women from Gaeta*
Spinning silk,
Silk and cotton.
Children, who do you like?
We like John

Who makes roosters sing,
The broody hen and the chicks,
Roosters and hens
That say cluck, cluck.
Sing, hen,
Lay an egg tomorrow morning
Near the red rooster
Close to the white one
That goes cockle-doodle-do.

Silk, money,
Women from Gaeta
Spinning silk,
They spin it too strong
And make doors shake.
Doors are of silver
And make five hundred
One hundred and fifty
The whole world sings.

The rooster sings
The hen answers.
Lady Columbine
Looked out of the window,
Three doves on her head.
Three foot soldiers pass by
On three white horses:
White saddle,
White damsel
White palfrey**.
Silk, money,
Women from Gaeta
Spinning silk
Silk and cotton ....

Children .... did you like it?

Notes

*A city in central Italy
**Note about Palfrey: "A palfrey is a type of horse highly valued as a riding horse in the Middle Ages. It is not a breed." -Wikipedia

FYI - "Moneta" can also be understood as "change"

Game Instructions

The way to play "Seta moneta" is with the child riding the adult's knees, the adult holds the child's hands and makes a push and pull saw movement.

Comments

This is a well-known version of Seta Moneta.

For more about Seta moneta, go to: http://www.mamalisa.com/?t=es&p=3101.

There, you'll find a video performance.

64

Seta moneta (Filastrocca) (Silk Money)

Seta moneta (Filastrocca)
(Italian Counting-out Rhyme)

Seta moneta,
Le donne di Gaeta*,
Che filano la seta,
La seta e la Cambagia** ;
Giovanni che mi piace,
Mi piace Giovanni,
Che fa cantare i galli,
Li galli e le galline,
Con tutti li pulcini.
Guardo nel pozzo
Che c'è un gallo rosso.
Guarda in quell' altro,
Che c'è un gallo bianco.
Guarda sul letto,
Che c'è un bel confetto.
Guarda lassù,
Che c'è un cuccurucù.

Silk Money
(English Translation)

Silk money,
The women of Gaeta*
Who spin silk,
Silk and cotton wool ;
Giovanni, that I like,
I like Giovanni,
Who makes the roosters sing,
The roosters and hens,
With all those chicks.
I look in the well,
What's there, a red rooster.
Look in that other one,
What's there, a white rooster.
Look on the bed,
What's there, a fine sugared almond

Look up there,
What's there, a cock-a-doodle-doo.

Notes

A city in central Italy
**"Cambagia" is a dialect term, for the Italian word, "bambagia", which in English is cotton wool.

Note: "Moneta" can also be understood as "change".

Game Instructions

The way to play "Seta moneta" is: with the child "riding" the adult's knees, the adult holds the child's hands and makes a push and pull "sawing" movement.

For more about Seta moneta (Filastrocca), go to:
http://www.mamalisa.com/?t=es&p=2101.

65

Sotto il ponte di Malacca (Under the Malacca Bridge)

This one's a bit gross, but it is a kids rhyme and that's how they often go. There are two versions of this rhyme. One is "Sotto il ponte di Malacca" and the other is "Sotto il ponte di Baracca" - the name of the bridge is different in each. You'll find both versions below.

Sotto il ponte di Malacca
(Italian Counting-out Song)

Sotto il ponte di Malacca
C'è zia che fa la cacca,
e la fa dura dura
il dottore la misura,
la misura a trenta tre
Donna, cavallo e re
Donna, cavallo e re*.

Under the Malacca Bridge
(English Translation)

Under the Malacca bridge,
There's Auntie making a poo,
And hard, so hard she does it.
The doctor measures it,
He measures it: thirty-three,
Queen, knight and king,
Queen, knight and king*.

Notes

* Reference to playing cards

Other Version:

SOTTO IL PONTE DI BARACCA

Sotto il ponte di Baracca
c'è Pierin che fa la cacca.
La fa dura, dura, dura,
il dottore la misura.
La misura trenta trè
uno, due, tre!

English Translation:

Under the Baracca Bridge

Under the Baracca bridge,
There's Little Johnie making a poo,
Hard, so hard he does it.
The doctor measures it,
He measures it: thirty-three,
One, two, three.

Game Instructions

Anna wrote, "This song is a game in which a child must sing a song counting out the children to see who starts the game. Counting out one child at a time, the last child to be counted out is the first to play!

'Il ponte di Malacca' is a bridge in Apulia; we used to sing the song to taunt the child who was named when singing!"

Comments

Gross rhymes are usually passed to the next generation far from parents' and teachers' ears.

For more about Sotto il ponte di Malacca, go to:
http://www.mamalisa.com/?t=es&p=2202.

There, you'll find a video performance.

66

Stella, stellina (Star, Little Star)

I asked Emanuela Marsura, a teacher in Italy, if they have an Italian version of Twinkle, Twinkle Little Star (http://www.mamalisa.com/?t=es&p=783&c=23) and she wrote: "We do not have a song like this. One that is a little like it might be 'Stella stellina'"...

Stella, stellina
(Italian Lullaby)

Stella, stellina,
La notte si avvicina.
La fiamma traballa.
La mucca nella stalla.
La mucca e il vitello,
La pecora e l'agnello,
La chioccia* con il pulcino,
Ognuno ha il suo bambino,
Ognuno ha la sua mamma,
E tutti fanno la nanna**!

Star, Little Star
(English Translation)

Star, little star,
Night is approaching.
The flame flickers.
The cow in the barn,
The cow and the calf,
The ewe and the lamb,
The hen* with the chick
Everyone has his child,
Everyone has his mother
And everyone went beddy-bye**.

Notes

Chioccia is a mother hen when she has hatching eggs and when she has chicks.
** Fare la nanna is baby talk for "to sleep", like "beddy bye" or "night night".

For more about Stella, stellina, go to: http://www.mamalisa.com/?t=es&p=2576.

There, you'll find sheet music, a MIDI melody and a video performance.

67

Sul tagliere l'aglio taglia (Cut the Garlic on the Cutting Board)

Sul tagliere l'aglio taglia
(Italian Tongue Twister)

Sul tagliere l'aglio taglia,
non tagliare la tovaglia.
La tovaglia non è aglio,
Se la tagli fai uno sbaglio.

Cut the Garlic on the Cutting Board
(English Translation)

Cut the garlic on the cutting board,
Do not cut the tablecloth.
The tablecloth is not garlic,
If you cut it, you made a mistake.

For more about Sul tagliere l'aglio taglia, go to:
http://www.mamalisa.com/?t=es&p=3331.

68

Tacci e taccin (Tacci and Taccin)

Tacci e taccin
(Italian Nursery Rhyme)

Tacci e taccin
faremo i tagliolin
per il babbo e per la mamma
per tutta la compagnia
questo bambino… buttalo via.

Tacci and Taccin
(English Translation)

Tacci and taccin*
We make noodles**
For daddy and mommy
For all our company.
This little boy, throw him away!

Notes

We think "tacci e taccin" means "staccia il staccio" in standard Italian = "the sifter sifts". We'd like to confirm this - if anyone has more information about this phrase, please email me. Thanks!

**The original is tagliolini which are noodles like spaghetti but a little thicker.*

Here's another version in the Romagnolo dialect:

Stacia e stacin

Stacia e stacin
che farem do taiolin
do per il babbo, do per la mamma
do per tut la compagnia
la Chiara buttala via!

English Translation:

The Sifter Sifts

The sifter sifts
So that we can make two noodles
Two for daddy, two for mommy
Two for all our company
Throw Claire (baby's name) away!

Comments

This rhyme can also be found in the online pdf in Italian Un mare di filastrocche
(http://gold.indire.it/datafiles/BDP-
GOLD000000000029E2DF/un%20mare%20di%20filastrocche,%20libro.pdf).

For more about Tacci e taccin, go to: http://www.mamalisa.com/?t=es&p=3288.

69

Tanti auguri a te (A Lot of Wishes for You)

Here's the Italian Birthday Song...

Tanti auguri a te
(Italian Birthday Song)

Tanti auguri a te
Tanti auguri a te
Tanti auguri (nome del bambino)
Tanti auguri a te.

A Lot of Wishes for You
(English Translation)

A lot of wishes for you
A lot of wishes for you
A lot of wishes for (child's name)
A lot of wishes for you.

For more about Tanti auguri a te, go to: http://www.mamalisa.com/?t=es&p=1276.

70

Te Didì (You Little Finger)

Gian sent this rhyme with the note: "This rhyme is in Bergamask (a Lombard dialect). This rhyme (as a lot of Italian rhymes) is not sung as a true song, but as a 'cantilena', as we say (I don't know the English word to describe it; the rhyme is sung as a sort of 'mantra')."

It sounds like this rhyme should be chanted. -Mama Lisa

Te Didì
(Italian Dialect Finger Play)

Te Didì va a tö 'l vi,
té Didà va a tö 'l pa,
te Celesta prepara la minestra,
te Lusea mètela ala 'ea,
e te Didù... cor an presù

You Little Finger
(English Translation)

You Little Finger go and buy wine,
You Ring Finger go and buy bread,
You Middle Finger* prepare the soup,
You Forefinger** cook it,
And you Thumb***... run to jail.

Notes

Here named Celesta
**Here called Lucy*
***In dialect didù, i.e. big finger*

*****

Standard Italian Translation
Tu Ditino

Tu Ditino (il mignolo) vai a comprare il vino,

tu Didà (l'anulare) vai a comprare il pane,
tu Celesta (il medio) prepara la minestra,
tu Lucia (l'indice) mettila sul fuoco
e tu Ditone (il pollice)... corri in prigione.

For more about Te Didì, go to: http://www.mamalisa.com/?t=es&p=2192.

71

Testa, spalle, ginocchia e piedi (Head, Shoulders, Knees and Feet)

Testa, spalle, ginocchia e piedi
(Italian Children's Song)

Testa, spalle, ginocchia e piedi
ginocchia e piedi.
Testa, spalle, ginocchia e piedi,
ginocchia e piedi.
Ho due occhi, un naso, una bocca e due orecchie,
testa, spalle, ginocchia e piedi,
ginocchia e piedi.

Head, Shoulders, Knees and Feet
(English Translation)

Head, shoulders, knees and feet,
knees and feet,
Head, shoulders, knees and feet,
knees and feet,
I have two eyes, a nose, a mouth and two ears,
Head, shoulders, knees and feet, knees and feet.

For more about Testa, spalle, ginocchia e piedi, go to:
http://www.mamalisa.com/?t=es&p=2561.

There, you'll find a video performance.

72

Topolino topoletto zum ba ba (Mousie, Mousey Zum Ba Ba)

Topolino topoletto zum ba ba
(Italian Handclapping Rhyme)

Topolino topoletto zum ba ba
si e ficato sotto il letto zum ba ba
e la mamma poveretta zum ba ba
li a tirato una scopetta zum ba ba
Corri corri a l'ospedale zum ba ba

l'ospedale era chiuso zum ba ba
corri corri a la farmacia zum ba ba
la farmacia era aperta zum ba ba
e li a meso una fascetta zum ba ba
piccolina piccoletta zul ba ba
topolino topoletto zum ba ba

Mousie, Mousey Zum Ba Ba
(English Translation)

Mousie, mousey* zum ba ba
Went under the bed zum ba ba
And mommy, poor dear, zum ba ba
Threw a broom at it zum ba ba
It ran, it ran to the hospital, zum ba ba
The hospital was closed zum ba ba
It ran, it ran to the pharmacy, zum ba ba
The pharmacy was open, zum ba ba
They put a bandage on it, zum ba ba
Tiny, shorty,** zum ba ba
Mousie, mousey zum ba ba.

Notes

*The Italian words are two diminutives of "mouse".
**The Italian words are two diminutives of "little".

For more about Topolino topoletto zum ba ba, go to:
http://www.mamalisa.com/?t=es&p=2769.

There, you'll find a video performance.

73

Trenta dì conta novembre (Thirty Days Has November)

This rhyme is for learning how many days there are in each month. It's like the English rhyme, Thirty Days Hath September (http://www.mamalisa.com/?t=hes&p=1366).

Trenta dì conta novembre
(Italian Nursery Rhyme)

Trenta dì conta novembre
con april, giugno e settembre.
Di ventotto ce n'è uno,
tutti gli altri ne han trentuno.

Thirty Days Has November
(English Translation)

Thirty days has November,
as with April, June and September,
with 28 there is one,
All the others have 31.

For more about Trenta dì conta novembre, go to:
http://www.mamalisa.com/?t=es&p=3286.

74

Trin' Trin', Cavallin' (Trot, Trot, Little Horse)

This song is in the Piedmontese Dialect...

Trin' Trin', Cavallin'
(Italian Dialect Nursery Rhyme)

Trin' Trin', Cavallin'
Sut' e' porte de Turin'
Sut' e' porte de Tortuna'
A' dua chi pistu l'erba buna.

Trot, Trot, Little Horse
(English Translation)

Trot, Trot, Little Horse,
Under the doorways of Turin,
Under the doorways of Tortona,
Where the good grass grows.

Notes

As I understood it, "Trin' Trin" is the sound the bells on the horse would make as he trots.

Game Instructions

Hold the baby sitting on your lap, riding your knees and make him/her bounce while you sing the rhyme.

Comments

Jacqueline Jill-Rito wrote, "This is a dialectical rhyme my maternal grandmother from Casale Monferrato (AL) used to sing to me as a child, in the Piedmontese dialect. I am now a teacher of Italian on the high school level on Long Island. During the summers I teach young children as an introduction to Italian. Thank you for your contribution to the rich culture of our heritage and a connection to our past."

Here's another version with a note sent by John Hannan:

Not really new, but a variant of Trin' Trin', Cavallin' that my mother remembers her father and uncles saying to her, also while bouncing on their knees. Not sure of the spelling but it sounded something like:

*Trotta Trotta Cavallin
Soua Joua Saint Martine*

And my mother's translation was:

*Trot Trot Little Horse
Up and back to St. Martin's.*

If anyone knows the correct spelling of this version, please email me. Thanks!

For more about Trin' Trin', Cavallin', go to:
http://www.mamalisa.com/?t=es&p=885.

75

Trotta, trotta, Bimbalotta (Trot, Trot, My Horse)

Marlene wrote: "I just found your site and am happy to contribute this little ditty that my grandmother sang to me. She was from San Matteo della Decima, northeast of Bologna, Italy. She came to the States in 1908 with her family, married a man from her village in Italy, and lived in Plymouth, Massachusetts.

The song is about a little horse named Bimbalotta, and I've written it phonetically in the dialect I heard as a child. I've also tried to translate it. It is usually sung to a baby while jostling the baby on one's lap, like 'Trot, Trot to Boston' and sung to the tune of the first verse of the 'Tarantella'."

Trotta, trotta, Bimbalotta
(Italian Dialect Children's Song)

Trotta, trotta, Bimbalotta,
Un furmai e no ricotta
Un parola tagliadelli
Tiala pungsa manganelli.

Trotta, trotta, mei caval,
Quand al veen della val,
Della val e del mouling,
Trotta, trotta, cavaling.

Trot, Trot, My Horse
(English Translation)

Trot, trot, my horse,
A cheese and not ricotta
A pan of tagliadelli*
Have a big belly full.

Trot, trot, my horse,
When you go in the valley,
In the valley and on the mountain,
Trot, trot, little horse.

Notes

A very thin spaghetti pasta

Note that "bimba" means "girl" or "baby girl" in Italian and "otta" can be used as a diminutive (to say it's the little version). So "bimbalotta" would be "little girl" or "little baby girl".

*****

The Italian book " Folklore emiliano raccolto a Cento" (1968) by Mario Borgatti has this version:

Trota trota, bimbalota,
un furmàj e una ricota,
un parol eel tajadèl
pr'impinir el to budèl '.

They give this translation in standard Italian:

Trotta, trotta, bimbalotta,
un formaggio e una ricotta,
un paiolo di tagliatelle
per riempire le tue budelle.

Here's an English translation by Mama Lisa:

Trot, trot, little girl,
Cheese and ricotta cheese,
A pot of noodles
To fill your belly.

Monique found the spelling below (this one can also be found on a menu in a restaurant in Bologna):

Trotta bimbalotta
un furmai e 'na ricotta
un parol ed taiadel
da impinir al mi budel.

It must mean:

Trot little child (little baby girl)
A cheese and a ricotta
A pan of tagliatelle
To fill my belly.

*****
Many times dialects have no authoritative written resources for proper spelling. We always welcome help fine-tuning the spelling of rhymes in dialects. Thanks! - Mama Lisa

For more about Trotta, trotta, Bimbalotta, go to:
http://www.mamalisa.com/?t=es&p=2706.

76

Trotta trotta cavallino (Trot, Trot Horsey)

Trotta trotta cavallino
(Italian Lap Rhyme)

Trotta trotta cavallino
per la strada del mulino;
il mulino non c'è più:
trotta trotta cadi giù!

Trot, Trot Horsey
(English Translation)

Trot, trot, horsey
on the road to the mill;
The mill is no longer there:
Trot, trot, fall down!

For more about Trotta trotta cavallino, go to:
http://www.mamalisa.com/?t=es&p=3341.

There, you'll find a video performance.

77

Trucci Trucci Cavallucci

Valentina wrote: " I would like to contribute this song my granny used to sing while letting us gallop on her legs. You sing it to a child who is seated on your lap, facing you, with legs apart, while holding his or her hands you gently move your thighs and knees up and down to mimic the galloping of a horse.

The lines are related in meaning to each other as each line asks a question about a word that has been mentioned in the preceding line. The "-" stands for a pause in singing.

The lyrics contain quite a variety of words, names of things, animals and onomatopoeia, very good for small children to learn; I still sing it to my 3 little girls and all their friends... Nursery rhymes are such a treasure that should not be forgotten!"

"Trucci trucci cavallucci" = Onomatopeic sounds. "Cavallucci" means little horses. "Clippity-clop, clippity-clop colts" is one translation into English that would keep the sense and the sounds of the words. -Mama Lisa.

Trucci Trucci Cavallucci
(Italian Nursery Rhyme)

Trucci trucci cavallu-cci:
chi è che va - a caval-lo
il re del Portogal-lo
con la cavalla zop-pa
chi l'ha zoppica-ta
la stanga della po-rta
dov'è la po-rta
l'ha bruciata il fuo-co
dov'è il fuo-co
l'ha spento l'a-cqua
dov'è l'a-cqua
l'ha bevuta il bu-e
dov'e il bu-e
il bue sta in campagna
e mangia noci
e castagna!

Trucci Trucci Cavallucci
(English Translation)

Trucci trucci cavallu-cci,
Who is it that is riding?
The king of Portugal
On a lame she-horse.
Who made her lame?
The door latch*.
Where is the door?
The fire has burnt it.
Where is the fire?
The water has put it out.
Where is the water?
The ox has drunk it.
Where is the ox?
The ox is in the country
And eats nuts
And chestnuts!

Notes

Normally a "stanga" is a door bar, the one you put across the door to keep it closed.

At the end you let the child bend his back away from you, by holding his/her hands, as if to let him fall, which usually causes great bursts of laughter!

*****
Here are the lyrics without the dashes:

Trucci trucci cavallucci
chi è che va a cavallo?
Il re del portogallo
con la cavalla zoppa.
Chi l'ha zoppicata?
La stanga della porta.
Dov'è la porta?
L'ha bruciata il fuoco!
Dov'è il fuoco?
L'ha spento l'acqua!
Dov'è l'acqua?
L'ha bevuta il bue
Dov'e il bue?
Il bue sta in campagna
e mangia noci
e castagna!

For more about Trucci Trucci Cavallucci, go to:
http://www.mamalisa.com/?t=es&p=2674.

78

Turli Turli piangeva (Turli Turli Was Crying)

Gerard sent this rhyme with the note: "I would like to submit this short item in remembrance of my mother Mamma Rosa Vernice di Corato la cantava spesso (from Corato, who often sang)... Of course my mother sang this to me often because I also wanted some chocolate. She also sang many of the songs that appear on your site."

Turli Turli piangeva
(Italian Children's Song)

Turli Turli piangeva
voleva la ciocolata
la mamma non aveva
Turli Turli piangeva

A mezzo giorno in punto
Passava un apparecchio
e sotto stava scritto
Turli Turli stai zitto.

Turli Turli Was Crying
(English Translation)

Turli Turli was crying
He wanted some chocolate
His mother did not have any
Turli Turli was crying.

At 12 o'clock exactly
An airplane was passing by
And underneath was written
Turli Turli be quiet.

Notes

Gian Carlo wrote me in March 2009, "I read on your website (I'm trying to read all the rhymes in your so interesting website) the children's song 'Turli Turli piangeva' and I remembered another version that my mother sang to me. In this version the child is called Pirulì (or, sometimes, Pirulìn) and doesn't eat chocolate, but a candle. Furthermore, the airplane doesn't pass by at twelve o'clock, but at midnight.

Pirulì Pirulì piangeva:
voleva la candela.
La mamma gliel' ha data
e lui se l'è mangiata

A mezzanotte in punto
passava un aeroplano
e sotto c'era scritto:
"Pirulì Pirulì sta zitto".

In English:

Pirulì Pirulì was crying:
He wanted a candle.
His mother gave it to him
And he ate it.

At midnight exactly
An airplane was passing by
And underneath was written:
Pirulì Pirulì be quiet.

Emanuela wrote in April 2011: "I know…

Pimpirulin piangeva,
voleva mezza mela.
La mamma non l'aveva,
Pimpirulin piangeva!

A mezzanotte in punto,
passa un aereoplano,
e sotto c'era scritto:
'Pimpirulin sta zitto!'.

English translation

Pimpirulin was crying,
He wanted half an apple.
The mom didn't have any,
Pimpirulin was crying!

At midnight on the dot,
An airplane passes,
And under it was written:
'Pimpirulin be quiet!'!"

For more about Turli Turli piangeva, go to:
http://www.mamalisa.com/?t=es&p=886.

There, you'll find sheet music, a MIDI melody and a video performance.

79

Tu scendi dalle stelle (You Come Down from the Stars)

Here's a beloved Italian Christmas Carol that has touched many people around the world...

Tu scendi dalle stelle
(Italian Christmas Carol)

Tu scendi dalle stelle
O Re del Cielo
E vieni in una grotta
Al freddo al gelo
E vieni in una grotta
Al freddo al gelo.

O Bambino mio Divino
Io ti vedo qui a tremar,
O Dio Beato!
Ah, quanto ti costò
L'avermi amato.
Ah, quanto ti costò
L'avermi amato.

A te che sei del mondo,
Il creatore,
Mancano panni e fuoco,
O mio Signore.
Mancano panni e fuoco,
O mio Signore.

Caro eletto pargoletto,
Quanto questa povertà
Più mi innamora,
Giacchè ti fece amor
Povero ancora.
Giacchè ti fece amor
Povero ancora.

You Come Down from the Stars
(English Translation)

You come down from the stars
Oh, King of Heavens,
And You come in a cave
in the cold, in the frost,
And You come in a cave
in the cold, in the frost.

Oh, my Divine Baby
I see you trembling here,
Oh, Blessed God
Ah, how much it costs You,
Your loving me.
Ah, how much it costs You,
Your loving me.

For You, who are for all the world
The creator,
No clothes and fire,
Oh, my Lord,
No clothes and fire,
Oh, my Lord.

Dear chosen one, little infant,
This dire poverty,
Makes me love You more,
Since Love made You
poor now,
Since Love made You
poor now.

Notes

*Tu scendi dalle stelle was composed by Saint Alfonso Maria de' Liguori, a
Neapolitan bishop, in 1754. The lyrics to this carol were originally in the
Neapolitan dialect. The carol was first called* QUANNO NASCETTE NINNO. *The
song was later re-written in Italian by Pope Pius IX and became a carol famous
all over the world.*

*****

*Come Check Out Mama Lisa's World Blog Post: Tu scendi dalle stelle (You Come
Down from the Stars): A Favorite Italian Christmas Carol with 2 YouTube Videos
(http://www.mamalisa.com/blog/?p=617).*

*****

Gian Carlo wrote about Tu scendi dalla stelle:

*...perhaps the oldest Christmas Song in Italy, ascribed to Sant'Alfonso Maria de'
Liguori (1696-1787), a catholic bishop, that wrote this song in 1755 in Nola
(Naples)... the song is longer than the lyrics above. This is the complete song:*

Tu scendi dalle stelle, o Re del cielo,

e vieni in una grotta al freddo e al gelo,
e vieni in una grotta al freddo e al gelo.
O Bambino mio divino,
io Ti vedo qui a tremar;
o Dio beato!
Ah, quanto Ti costò l'avermi amato!
Ah, quanto Ti costò l'avermi amato!

A Te, che sei del mondo il Creatore,
mancano panni e fuoco, o mio Signore,
mancano panni e fuoco, o mio Signore.
Caro eletto pargoletto,
quanto questa povertà
più m'innamora,
giacché Ti fece amor povero ancora,
giacché Ti fece amor povero ancora.

Tu lasci il bel gioir del divin seno,
per giunger a penar su poco fieno,
per giunger a penar su poco fieno.
Dolce amore del mio core,
dove amore Ti trasportò?
O Gesù mio,
perché tanto patir? Per amor mio!
Perché tanto patir? Per amor mio!

Ma se fu Tuo volere il Tuo patire,
perché vuoi pianger poi, perché vagire?
Perché vuoi pianger poi, perché vagire?
Mio Gesù, T'intendo sì!
Ah, mio Signore!
Tu piangi non per duol, ma per amore.
Tu piangi non per duol, ma per amore.

Tu piangi per vederti da me ingrato
dove sì grande amor, sì poco amato!
O diletto del mio petto,
Se già un tempo fu così,
or Te sol bramo.
Caro non pianger più, ch'io T'amo e T'amo,
caro non pianger più, ch'io T'amo e T'amo.

Tu dormi, Ninno mio, ma intanto il core
non dorme, no, ma veglia a tutte l'ore.
Deh, mio bello e puro Agnello
a che pensi? Dimmi tu.
O amore immenso!
"Un dì morir per Te", rispondi, "io penso".
"Un dì morir per Te", rispondi, "io penso".

Dunque a morire per me, Tu pensi, o Dio:
e chi altro, fuor di Te, amar poss'io?
O Maria, speranza mia,
se poc'amo il Tuo Gesù,

non Ti sdegnare.
Amalo tu per me, s'io nol so amare!
Amalo tu per me, s'io nol so amare!

English Translation

You come down from the stars
Oh, King of Heaven,
And You come to a cave in the cold and frost.
And You come to a cave in the cold and frost.
Oh, my Divine Child
I see You trembling here,
Oh, Blessed God
Ah, how much it cost You loving me.
Ah, how much it cost You loving me.

For You, who is the creator of the world,
No clothes and fire, oh my Lord,
No clothes and fire, oh my Lord.
Dear Chosen little baby,
So much deprivation,
Makes me love You more,
Since Love made You more poor,
Since Love made You more poor.

You leave the beautiful glory of the divine bosom,
To come suffer on a little hay,
To come suffer on a little hay.
Sweet love of my heart,
Where did love carry You?
O my Jesus.
Why do You suffer so much? Because You love me.
Why do You suffer so much? Because You love me.

But if your suffering was Your will,
Why, afterwards, do You wish to weep? Why are You crying?
My Jesus, I understand you, yes!
Ah, my Lord!
You are weeping not because of pain, but because of love,
You are weeping not because of pain, but because of love.

You are crying because You see me ungrateful,
Whence such great love, so little beloved!
Oh, beloved of my breast,
If previously it was this way,
Now I love only You.
Dear, don't cry anymore, since I love You, and I love You.
Dear, don't cry anymore, since I love You, and I love You.

You sleep, my child, but meanwhile the heart
Is not sleeping, but is always awake.
Ah, my beautiful and pure lamb,
What are You thinking of? Tell me.
Oh, immense love!

"I think one day I'll die for you," You reply.
"I think one day I'll die for you," You reply.

So You are thinking of dying for me, my God:
Who else, besides you, can I love?
Oh Mary, my hope,
If I love your Jesus so little,
Don't be outraged.
Love him for me, if I am not able to love Him!
Love him for me, if I am not able to love Him!

For more about Tu scendi dalle stelle, go to:
http://www.mamalisa.com/?t=es&p=1313.

There, you'll find sheet music, a MIDI melody and a video performance.

Un elefante si dondolava (One Elephant was Swinging)

Un elefante si dondolava
(Italian Children's Song)

Un elefante si dondolava
sopra il filo di una ragnatela,
e ritenendo la cosa interessante
andò a chiamare un altro elefante.

Due elefanti si dondolavano
sopra il filo di una ragnatela
e ritenendo la cosa interessante
andarono a chiamare un altro elefante.

Tre elefanti si dondolavano
sopra il filo di una ragnatela
e ritenendo la cosa interessante
andarono a chiamare un altro elefante.

Quattro elefanti...

One Elephant was Swinging
(English Translation)

One elephant was swinging
On the thread of a spider web
And considering how appealing it was
He went to call another elephant.

Two elephants were swinging
On the thread of a spider web
And considering how appealing it was
They went to call another elephant.

Three elephants were swinging
On the thread of a spider web
And considering how appealing it was
They went to call another elephant.

Four elephants…

For more about Un elefante si dondolava, go to:
http://www.mamalisa.com/?t=es&p=3335.   .

81

Uno, Due, Tre (One, Two, Three)

Uno, Due, Tre
(Italian Children's Song)

Uno, due, tre,
La Peppina fa il caffè.
Fa il caffè di cioccolata!
La Peppina i'enamorata.

One, Two, Three
(English Translation)

One, two, three,
Peppina is making coffee.
She makes coffee out of chocolate!
Peppina is in love.

For more about Uno, Due, Tre, go to: http://www.mamalisa.com/?t=es&p=889.

82

Un pezzo di pizza (A Piece of Pizza)

Un pezzo di pizza
(Italian Tongue Twister)

Un pezzo di pizza
che puzza nel pozzo
del pazzo di pezza.

A Piece of Pizza
(English Translation)

A piece of pizza
That's stinks in the sewer*
Of the madman in rags.

Notes

Literally, "well"

For more about Un pezzo di pizza, go to:
http://www.mamalisa.com/?t=es&p=3330.

83

Vinni la primavera (Spring Has Come)

This song is also known as "Si maritau Rosa"

Vinni la primavera
(Sicilian Dialect Folk Song)

Vinni la primavera
li mennuli su n'ciuri
Lu focu di l'ammuri
lu cori m'addumò.
E ammezzu suli e ciuri,
avvolunu l'aceddi
Tutti 'sti cosi beddi
mi fannu suspirà.

(Ritornello)
Si maritau Rosa
Saridda e Pippinedda
e iù, ca sugnu bedda
mi vogghiu marità.
Si maritau Rosa
Saridda e Pippinedda
Pi ia cha sognu bedda
maritau non cin'è.

Tanti picciotti beddi
passunu di sta' strata;
ma nuddu 'na vardata
alla mé casa dà.
Certu 'stu desideriu
distruggi la mé vita
mi vogghiu fari zita
mi vogghiu marità.

(Ritornello)

La dota l'àiu fatta
la casa l'àiu macari
schetta non vogghiu stari
rannuzza sugnu già
La culpa è di mé matri
mi teni arritirata

ma ora la iurnata
vaiu di ccà e di ddà.

(Ritornello)

Spring Has Come
(English Translation)

Spring has come
The almond trees are in bloom
And the fire of love
Has awoken in my heart.
Amidst the sun and flowers,
Little birds are flying
All of these beautiful things
Make me sigh.

(Chorus)
Rosa got married,
and Sara and Josephine,
and I who am beautiful,
I want to get married too.
Rosa got married
and Sara and Josephine,
But I who am beautiful
I am not married.

So many handsome guys
Walk down this street;
But not even a glance
Do they give to my house.
Certainly this desire
Is destroying my life,
I want to get engaged
I want to get married.

(Chorus)

My dowry is ready,
A house as well,
I don't want to stay single
I am already a bit old.
It's my mother's fault
She kept me at home too much
But now all day long
I go here and there.

(Chorus)

Notes

There are different versions of this song.

Comments

"A traditional love song known all over Sicily, with a waltz rhythm..." -Italy World Club (http://www.italyworldclub.com/italian-songs/regional/sicilia/si-maritau-rosa.htm)

For more about Vinni la primavera, go to:
http://www.mamalisa.com/?t=es&p=3365.

There, you'll find **a video performance.**

Thanks and Acknowledgements!

We're so grateful to everyone who helped us gather the material for this book. We particularly wish to thank Ernestine Shargool (www.proz.com/profile/812677), Gian Carlo Macchi, and Emanuela Marsura for their many contributions. And thanks to Mama Lisa's daughter and her friends and also to Gracie Gralike for their wonderful drawings. Grazie!

1 A bi bo (A Be Bow)
Translation: Mama Lisa and Monique

Photo: Mama Lisa

2 Arre, arre, cavalluccio (Giddy-up, Giddy-up Horsey)
Many thanks to Melissa for contributing and translating this nursery rhyme.

3 Aulì ulè
Many thanks to Gian Carlo Macchi for contributing this rhyme!

4 Avete paura dell'uomo nero? (Are you Afraid of the Bogeyman?)
Many thanks to Emanuela Marsura for contributing this game with the translation and commentary!

5 Batta le Manine (Clap Your Hands)
Many thanks to Nicole Midura for contributing and translating this "hand clapping song" in January 2005. Many thanks also to Nadia for sending us an alternate version of it. Many thanks also to Rino for the third version. Thanks to Anna Calise for the 4th version. Thanks to Adriana Baratta for the 5th version.

6 Batti manuzzi (Clap Your Little Hands)
Many thanks to Toni C. for contributing this "hand clapping song" and for translating it in both English and standard Italian.

Thanks to Marisa Roche for the drawing!

7 Bobo la bilancia (Bobo the Scale)
Thanks to Janet for sending us this rhyme! Translation by Lisa and Monique.

8 Bolli bolli pentolino (Boil, Boil, Little Pot)
Many thanks to Sarina Longin for the drawing!

9 Capra Capretta (Goat, Little Goat)
Translation: Mama Lisa and Tatie Monique

Thanks to Lila Pomerantz for the drawing of Salt!

10 Centocinquanta (One Hundred and Fifty)
Many thanks also to Emanuela Marsura for contributing this song. Translated by Emanuela, Monique and Lisa.

Thanks to Lila Pomerantz for the drawing!

11 C'era una volta un Re (There Once Was a King)
Translation: Mama Lisa

Thanks to Lila Pomerantz for the drawing of "C'era una volta un Re" (There Once Was a King).

12 Chi beddu stu cappiduzzu (How Beautiful is this Hat)
Many thanks to Ann Mancini for contributing and translating this song with her Mom, Dorothy Dietrich (the song was taught to her by her grandmother, Maria Ferrantelli).

13 Cimene, Cimene (Chimney, Chimney)
Many thanks to Lois Erskine for contributing and translating this song and for sharing her little stories.

14 Cincirinella
Thanks to Ernestine Shargool for contributing and translating this song. Many thanks also to Maria Sabatino-Cabardo for contributing, translating the 2nd version into standard Italian and to Monique Palomares for translating it into English. Many thanks to Nick Ferrara for contributing and translating the additional verse.

15 Dice il pollice (The Thumb Says)
Many thanks to Emanuela for contributing and translating the 1st version of this song and to Anna Calise for the 2nd version.

Thanks to Sarina Longin for the drawing of the hand!

16 Din, Don, Campanon (Ding, Dong, Big Bell's Tones)
Many thanks to Ernestine Shargool for contributing and translating this song.

Literal translation by Monique Palomares.

18 Don don Dalena (Dong Dong Dalena)
Many thanks to Gayle Hess for contributing and translating this nursery rhyme.

19 Dormi fili, dormi! (Sleep Son, Sleep!)
English Translation by Lisa Yannucci and Monique Palomares. Many thanks to Jean-Paul Lacombe for helping with the translation into French.

20 Fa la ninna, fa la nanna (Go to Sleep, Go to Sleepy)
Many thanks to Gilbert DeBenedetti, webmaster and musical arranger of the website G Major Music Theory (http://www.gmajormusictheory.org/), for contributing and translating this song, and for the midi tune and score.

21 Farfallina (Butterfly)
Many thanks to Nicole Midura, Lois Erskine, Nina and Lisa (Presutti) TerKeurst for contributing and translating the four different versions of this song. (The version with two verses above was submitted by Lisa Terkeurst.)

Thanks to Gracie for the wonderful illustration!

22 Filastrocca della settimana (The Days of the Week Rhyme)
Translated by Lisa Yannucci and Monique Palomares.

23 Filastrocca senza senso - Ambarabai ciccì coccò (Nonsense Rhyme)
Many thanks to Gian Carlo Macchi for contributing and translating this song and for such interesting commentary about it.

24 Fra' Martino (Frère Jacques)
Many thanks to Ernestine Shargool for contributing this song.

Translation by Monique and Lisa

25 Funiculì, Funiculà
The photo of the funicular of Mt. Vesuvius at the top of the page is from Mt. Vesuvius Online (http://www.vesuvioinrete.it/e_index.htm).

26 Gesù bambino (Baby Jesus)
Translation: Mama Lisa

27 Giro, Giro, Tondo (Turn, Turn Around)

Many thanks to Lina A. Bosco for providing the words and translation for this song. Thanks also to Thanks to Alfredo Parra for contributing the midi music and to Annalisa and Sanam Dabiri for the 2nd version of GIRO GIRO TONDO. Thanks to Anna Simonetti for the 3rd version. Thanks to Monique for the 4th translation.

28 Il cavallo del bambino (The Child's Horse)
Contributed and translated by Monique Palomares.

30 La Befana vien di notte (The Befana Comes at Night)
Many thanks to Maria Sabatino-Cabardo for sending the alternate version of the rhyme

31 La bella lavanderina (The Pretty Washerwoman)
Translation: Mama Lisa

32 La gallina (The Hen)
Many thanks to Sandrine Quinchon for contributing this song. Translated by Monique Palomares and Lisa Yannucci. Thanks to Jadwiga Andrychowska-Biegacz for helping with the score.

33 Lalla, Lalla, Lalla
This lullaby was found in a scholium (early commentary) on Persius.

34 La luna (The Moon)
Translated by Lisa Yannucci

35 Le ciotoline (The Little Bowls)
Many thanks to Gian Carlo Macchi for contributing and translating this song, for the recording and the musical score. Thank you for sharing this special song with us Gian Carlo. -Lisa

36 Lucciola, Lucciola (Firefly, Firefly)
Many thanks to Ernestine Shargool for contributing and translating this song. Many thanks also to Gian Carlo Macchi for contributing the Lombardy version.

37 Mamma mia, dammi cento lire (Mom, Give Me A Hundred Pounds)
Many thanks also to Emanuela Masura for contributing this song and an English translation.

38 Mano, mano morta (Hand, Dead Hand)
Many thanks to Claudia for contributing this rhyme. Many thanks also to Lucia Bini for contributing and translating the second version of it. Many thanks also to Rosa Cotrona for contributing and translating the third version of it.
Sicilian and Venetian versions contributed and translated by Monique Palomares.

Thanks to Lila Pomerantz for the drawing of Mano Morta!

39 Maramao
Many thanks to Ernestine Shargool for contributing and translating this song. Ernestine learnt this rhyme from her mother (Neapolitan) but many variations exist in different dialects.

40 Maria lavava (Mary Busy with the Washing)
Many thanks to Ernestine Shargool for contributing and translating this song.

41 Micio Miagolio (Kitty Cat)
Many thanks to my grandmother, Maria Yannucci, for reciting and translating this song, to JoyceAnna DiSclafani for providing the Italian version and to Nicoletta DeJoseph for sending the spelling in the dialect.

Thanks to Lila Pomerantz for the drawing!

42 Mie Mama Mata Mata (Coo-roo, Coo-roo)
Many thanks to Ernestine Shargool for contributing and translating this song.

43 Milano Torino (Milan Turin)
Many thanks to Anna Simonetti from Foggia, Italy, for contributing this song.

44 Nanna cunetta (As You're Sleeping in Your Bed)
Many thanks to Joe Daly for contributing and translating this song.

45 Nella vecchia fattoria (On the Old Farm)
Many thanks to Victoria Alliegro for contributing this song. Many thanks also to Kelly for contributing and translating the second version of this song. Translations edited by Lisa Yannucci.

46 Ninna nanna a sette e venti (Lullaby At Twenty Past Seven)
Many thanks to Gian Carlo Macchi for contributing and translating this song and for the recording.

47 Ninnananna di Fra' Simon (Brother Simon's Lullaby)
Many thanks to Alfredo Parra for contributing the words, music and translation for this lullaby.

48 Ninnananna di Gesù Bambino (Infant Jesus' Lullaby)
Many thanks to Alfredo Parra for contributing the words, sheet music and translation for this lullaby.

49 Ninna nanna, ninna oh (Lullaby, Lullaby, ooh)
Many thanks to Sandrine Quinchon for contributing this song. Translated by Monique Palomares and Lisa Yannucci.

Many thanks also to Toni MacNeish for the second version of this song.

Thanks to Emanuela Marsura for commenting on this song.

50 Oh che bel castello (Oh, What a Fine Castle)
Many thanks to Monique Palomares for contributing this song. Translated by Monique and Lisa.

Thanks to Melisa Roche for the drawing!

51 Oh veni, sonnu (Oh Come Sleep)
Many thanks to Gian Carlo Macchi for contributing and translating these songs.

52 Peppina prendi un pettine (Peppina, Get a Comb)
Translation: Mama Lisa

53 Personent hodie (This Day Resounds)
First translation: Lisa Yannucci

54 Piazza bella piazza (Plaza, Pretty Plaza)
Many thanks to Monique Palomares for contributing this finger play. Translated by Monique and Lisa.

55 Piva piva l'oli d'uliva (Piva, Piva, Olive Oil)
Many thanks to Gian Carlo Macchi for contributing and translating this song, for the photos and for such interesting commentary.

56 Prezzemolo in mezzo (Parsley Put Itself in the Middle)
Many thanks to Anna Simonetti (from Foggia) for contributing this song and to Emanuela Marsura for helping with the translation.

57 Questo l'occhio bello (This One, The Beautiful Eye)
Many thanks to Lisa Meier for contributing this song. Thanks to Melisa Roche for the drawing!

58 San Nicolò de Bari (Saint Nicholas of Bari)
Translated by Monique Palomares.

59 Santa Lucia

Many thanks to Gian Carlo Macchi for sending us this song and translation (translated with Lisa Yannucci).

Photo: Wikipedia (http://en.wikipedia.org/wiki/File:Sommer,_Giorgio_%281834-1914%29_-_n._11xx_-_Napoli,_S._Lucia_e_Hotel_de_Rome.jpg)

60 Sedia, sediola (Chair, Little Chair)
Many thanks to Valentina for contributing this song and the instructions.

61 Sega sega mastu Ciccio (Saw Saw, Master Ciccio)
Many thanks to Joann DellAversano for contributing this song. Thanks to Monique Palomares for translating it. Thanks to Adriana for the longer version.

62 Se sei felice tu lo sai (If You're Happy and You Know It)
Many thanks to Kelly Quinn for contributing this song. Thanks also to Monique Palomares for creating the midi tune. Thanks to Lila Pomerantz for the drawing!

63 Seta moneta (Silk Money)
Many thanks to Emanuela for contributing this song. Translated by Monique Palomares.

Thanks to Lila Pomerantz for the drawing!

64 Seta moneta (Filastrocca) (Silk Money)
This rhyme can be found in THE COUNTING-OUT RHYMES OF CHILDREN (1888), by Henry Carrington Bolton. Translated by Lisa Yannucci and Monique Palomares.

65 Sotto il ponte di Malacca (Under the Malacca Bridge)
Many thanks to Anna Simonetti from Foggia, Italy, for contributing this song.

66 Stella, stellina (Star, Little Star)
Many thanks to Emanuela Marsura for contributing this song with an English translation.

67 Sul tagliere l'aglio taglia (Cut the Garlic on the Cutting Board)
Translation: Mama Lisa and Tatie Monique

68 Tacci e taccin (Tacci and Taccin)
Many thanks to Dave Helmick for pointing out this rhyme.

Translated by Lisa Yannucci and Monique Palomares.

69 Tanti auguri a te (A Lot of Wishes for You)

Many thanks to Antoinette Candotti and Orsola for contributing this song.

Translated by Mama Lisa.

70 Te Didì (You Little Finger)
Many thanks to Gian Carlo Macchi for contributing and translating this rhyme.

71 Testa, spalle, ginocchia e piedi (Head, Shoulders, Knees and Feet)
Many thanks to Irene for contributing this song.

72 Topolino topoletto zum ba ba (Mousie, Mousey Zum Ba Ba)
Many thanks to Anna Simonetti for contributing this song and to Monique Palomares for the translation.

Drawings by Lila Pomerantz and Sarina Longin.

73 Trenta dì conta novembre (Thirty Days Has November)
Translated by Lisa Yannucci

74 Trin' Trin', Cavallin' (Trot, Trot, Little Horse)
Many thanks to Jacqueline Jill-Rito for contributing and translating this song. Thanks to John Hannan for the second version.

Thanks to Sarina Longin for the drawing!

75 Trotta, trotta, Bimbalotta (Trot, Trot, My Horse)
Many thanks to Marlene Brigida Baldwin for contributing and translating this song.

76 Trotta trotta cavallino (Trot, Trot Horsey)
Translated by Mama Lisa and Tatie Monique.

77 Trucci Trucci Cavallucci
Many thanks to Valentina for contributing and translating this nursery rhyme.

78 Turli Turli piangeva (Turli Turli Was Crying)
Many thanks to Gerard Vernice for contributing and translating this song. Many thanks to Gian Carlo Macchi for contributing and translating the second version of this song and for helping with the midi and score. Many thanks to Emanuela Marsura for contributing and translating the third version.

79 Tu scendi dalle stelle (You Come Down from the Stars)
English Translations: Gian Carlo Macchi, Monique Palomares and Lisa Yannucci. Midi Music: Monique.

Many thanks also to Gian Carlo Macchi for contributing the complete song.

80 Un elefante si dondolava (One Elephant was Swinging)
Translated by Mama Lisa.

81 Uno, Due, Tre (One, Two, Three)
Many thanks to Joe Daly for contributing and translating this song. Thanks to Sanam Dabiri for contributing this song too!

82 Un pezzo di pizza (A Piece of Pizza)
Translation: Mama Lisa

83 Vinni la primavera (Spring Has Come)
Thanks to Johanna Kreisler for contributing this song!

Translated by Lisa and Monique.

About Mama Lisa's World

Mama Lisa's World (www.mamalisa.com) is the internet's premier destination for children's songs from around the globe and for discussions of international culture. It features thousands of traditional songs from over a hundred countries and cultures and a major collection of Mother Goose Rhymes. Mama Lisa's Blog focuses on global recipes, holiday traditions, poetry and lively conversations about childhood around the world.

About the Staff

Lisa Yannucci (Mama Lisa)
Lisa was inspired to start Mama Lisa's World in the mid 1990's, when her young son first became interested in nursery rhymes. She recorded several Mother Goose songs onto a computer and programmed them to play when he clicked a picture. He loved it and she became fascinated with the power of the internet to enrich the lives of children. She made the site public and has since used her background in languages and culture, and her talent as an illustrator, to oversee its tremendous growth.

Jason Pomerantz
Jason (Lisa's husband) has worked in magazine, book and web publishing for over twenty years. His personal projects have included several websites and podcasts. Along with his editorial contributions, he oversees the business and technical aspects of Mama Lisa's World.

Monique Palomares
Monique grew up at the crossroads of three cultures in the Occitan region of France. She is fluent in French, Spanish, English and Occitan and has a working knowledge of many other languages including Italian. Her years as a first grade teacher and her love of children and linguistics give her a unique insight into the power of music and song all over the world.

About You

Mama Lisa's World is made up of contributions from ordinary people from all over the globe. Please visit us at www.mamalisa.com and say hello! We want to hear about your childhood memories, your favorite recipes, your holidays and anything else you'd like to share about your culture.

Thank you for being part of our community!

21159697R00106

Made in the USA
San Bernardino, CA
02 January 2019